Countering Jihadi Cool

The Fairleigh Dickinson University Press
Series in Law, Culture, and the Humanities

Series Editor: Caroline Joan "Kay" S. Picart, M.Phil. (Cantab), Ph.D., J.D.-M.A., Esquire
Appellate Assistant Public Defender, FL 10th Jud. Cir., former adjunct professor of law, FAMU, former professor of Philosophy, English & Humanities, FSU

The Fairleigh Dickinson University Press Series in Law, Culture, and the Humanities publishes scholarly works in which the field of Law intersects with, among others, Film, Criminology, Sociology, Communication, Critical/Cultural Studies, Literature, History, Philosophy, and the Humanities.
On the Web at http://www.fdu.edu/fdupress

Publications

Caroline Joan "Kay" S. Picart, *Countering Jihadi Cool: Narrative, Law, Culture, and Philosophy Against Global Jihad* (2025)
Peter Robson, *Rumpole and His Rivals: Comic Legal Fiction* (2025)
Vincenzo Tomeo and Peter Robson (translator), *The Judge on the Screen: A Translation and Critical Edition* (2024)
Kevin S. Jobe, *Malevolent Legalities: Discriminatology and the Specters of Scalia* (2024)
Linda Myrsiades, *From Treason to Runaway Slaves: Legal Culture in New Republic Trials, 1783–1808* (2023)
Eamon P. H. Keane and Peter Robson, *The Ian Willock Collection on Law and Justice in the Twenty-First Century* (2023)
Peter Robson and Ferdinando Spina, *Vigilante Justice in Society and Popular Culture: A Global Perspective* (2022)
Joel Silverman, *The Legal Exhibitionist: Morris Ernst, Jewish Identity, and the Modern Celebrity Lawyer* (2022)
Matthew Sorrento and David Ryan, *David Fincher's* Zodiac*: Cinema of Investigation and (Mis)Interpretation* (2021)
T. Patrick Hill, *No Place for Ethics: Judicial Review, Legal Positivism, and the Supreme Court of the United States* (2021)
Caroline Joan "Kay" S. Picart, *Monsters, Law, Crime: Explorations in Gothic Criminology* (2020)
Elaine Wood, *Gender Justice and the Law: Theoretical Practices of Intersectional Identity* (2020)
Orit Kamir, *Betraying Dignity: The Toxic Seduction of Social Media, Shaming, and Radicalization* (2019)
Marouf A. Hasian, Jr., *Lawfare and the Ovaherero and Nama Pursuit of Restorative Justice, 1918–2018* (2019)
George Pate, *Enter the Undead Author: Intellectual Property, the Ideology of Authorship, and Performance Practices since the 1960s* (2019)

Countering Jihadi Cool

Narrative, Law, Culture, and Philosophy Against Global Jihad

Caroline Joan "Kay" S. Picart

FAIRLEIGH DICKINSON UNIVERSITY PRESS
Vancouver • Madison • Teaneck • Wroxton

Published by Fairleigh Dickinson University Press
Copublished by BLOOMSBURY ACADEMIC
Bloomsbury Publishing Inc, 1359 Broadway, 12th floor, New York, NY 10018, USA
Bloomsbury Publishing Plc, 50 Bedford Square, London, WC1B 3DP, UK
Bloomsbury Publishing Ireland, 29 Earlsfort Terrace, Dublin 2, D02 AY28, Ireland

First published in the United States of America 2025

Fairleigh Dickinson University Press gratefully acknowledges the support received for scholarly publishing from the Friends of FDU Press.

Library of Congress Control Number: 2025938445

ISBN: HB: 978-1-68393-438-7
PB: 978-1-68393-440-0
ePDF: 978-1-68393-705-0
eBook: 978-1-68393-617-6

Typeset by Deanta Global Publishing Services, Chennai, India

To Jerry Rivera, the love of my life, my shelter through life's storms, my husband, lover, and beloved whose purity of passion and strength of compassion render every moment meaningful. May silence speak where words slip, slide, and perish.

Contents

Acknowledgments

Parts of this book have been published as a law review article: "Countering Jihadi Cool and the Case of Raza v. City of New York," 12 *Indiana Journal of Law and Social Equality* 2 (Spring 2024), 209–48. I am grateful to the staff of the *Indiana Journal of Law and Social Equality* for their helpful input on an earlier version of Chapter 2, on the case of *Raza v. City of New York*.

The description of Jihadi Cool/Chic appeared in an earlier form and has been adapted with permission from Cambridge Scholars Publishing. It first appeared in *American Lone Work Terrorists and the Allure of Jihadi Cool/Chic: Colleen Larose and the Tsarnaev Brothers* (Cambridge Scholars' Publishing, 2017).

The project of developing a poethics of witnessing was first explored in "Nationalities, Histories, Rhetorics: Real/Reel Representations of the Holocaust and Holocaust Trials and a Poethics of Film and Law," 29 *Dapim: Studies on the Holocaust* 2, 1–20 (May, 2015); doi: 10.1080/23256249.2015.1034980 . I thank the journal for permission to adapt the material to this new manuscript.

The study of the roles the internet plays in self-radicalization was first explored in "'Jihad Cool/Jihad Chic': The Roles of the Internet and Imagined Relations in the Self-Radicalization of Colleen LaRose" (Jihad Jane), *Societies*, 5 (April 2015): 354–383; doi: 10.3390/soc5020354. I have retained copyright to this article. "© 2024 by the authors; licensee MDPI, Basel, Switzerland. This article [was] an open access article distributed under the terms and conditions of the Creative Commons Attribution License (http://creativecommons.org/licenses/by/4.0/)."

I am very grateful for the encouragement and support of numerous colleagues, such as Harry Keyishian, Charles Courtney, James Brummer, Berta Hernandez-Truyol, Danaya Wright, and Randy Abate, among so many others. I am also very grateful for the constructive and encouraging commentary provided by an anonymous reader.

I am also indebted to my colleagues at the appellate division of the Florida Tenth Judicial Circuit, Public Defender's Office, and especially Lisa Lott and Blair Allen, whose support in my continuing to pursue my academic and artistic interests beyond legal work have been invaluable. All views expressed in this book are the author's views and do not represent the official position of the Florida Tenth Judicial Circuit Public Defender's Office.

This book would not have been completed without the patient and expert assistance of Margaret Baker-Petty, who assisted with the final formatting and indexing of the book. Zach Nycum, editor at Bloomsbury, and the editorial staff provided efficient and helpful assistance in getting the book production-ready.

Finally, I am truly blessed to have the support of my husband and love of my life, Gerardo "Jerry" Rivera, my daughter, Jessie, and my grandson, Joey; my surrogate parents, Jim and Carolyn Terrell; and my siblings, Richard Picart, Blanche Canio, and Yvette Picart-Oliveros, and their families. Everything I accomplish, I attribute, in loving memory, to my parents, Drs. Robert and Anarose Picart.

For all Graces and Blessings, I am always deeply grateful to God the Father, Son and Holy Spirit.

Foreword

Harry Keyishian

Professor Emeritus of English, Fairleigh Dickinson University

By tracing the ways in which individuals are recruited into terrorist activities through social media, Dr. Caroline Picart provides both a chilling account of recent events and an acute analysis of their causes, effects, and costs, both social and personal. Recognizing the acute differences between modern jihadists and those of the past, she explores the frightening phenomenon of self-radicalization through the internet. To this acute analysis, she adds, in this work especially, strategies for countering such phenomena as "jihadi cool" and "jihadi chic" that have effectively recruited to violent causes so many young people wishing to give meaning to their lives. To avoid misleading generalizations, she differentiates between Salafism, which follows the letter of Islamic law and tries to convince through example and teaching, and Jihadism, which looks on violence as an individual obligation. A new phenomenon, which she terms Salafi-Jihadism, melds the two by creating a clearer rationale for, and a more direct path toward, violence. These understandings are vital to mounting effective counter-jihadi strategies and for confronting the problems associated with self-radicalization. Dr. Picart's account of Yazidi genocide by ISIS reveals the tragedy and terror of violence practiced outside the guiderails of conscience. She ends with a subtle and searching set of strategies for countering the terrorist narrative, based on "a return to the cultures/narratives of human dignity and respect" and asks that we seek more effective and keener understandings of the norms that encourage virtual connectedness. Her study sheds light on some of the darkest episodes of violence in our era and, through keen, informed analysis, offers us ways to comprehend and confront them. It is important work and a significant addition to our knowledge and understanding of the destructive forces alive in the world today.

1

The Rhetoric and Aesthetic of "Jihadi Cool/Chic"

Overview: Surveying the Shifting Terrain

This book springs from a confluence of factors, including the proliferation of both domestic and global instances of terrorism, inclusive of: (1) the development of "self-radicalizing terrorists" linked to internet activity, (2) the allure of a virtual culture of "jihadi cool" or "jihadi chic," which has become a powerful recruitment tool of some terrorist groups and its evolution and propagation through mediated artifacts, and (3) the emergence of a variety of national and international efforts, initiated by different actors, both governmental and nongovernmental, aimed at countering or demythologizing the culture of jihadi cool/chic.

While recognizing that combating global terrorism inevitably and pragmatically entails sustained and ever-evolving military efforts and policy adaptations, this book limits its scope to selected legal and cultural instances of such counter-jihadi cool efforts. Specifically, this book, on the one hand, focuses both on the cultural and social bases that undergird the persuasive appeal of jihadi cool and on the persistence of domestic and global terrorism. On the other hand, it also critically analyzes whether radicalization theory, which has been theoretically debunked, actually continues to inform current police practices.

Indeed, there appears to be an emerging consensus among counter-terrorism analysts and practitioners that there is a pressing exigency to move beyond security and intelligence measures. There is an urgent need to enact, to the extent possible, proactive measures to prevent potentially vulnerable individuals from self-radicalizing or perhaps to rehabilitate those who ha previously been drawn in by the allure of jihadi cool.[1] Nevertheless, as in C. S. Lewis's *Perelandra*, perhaps it is best to visualize what is possible as a shifting, undulating milieu rather than as a static ground. As Greg C. Reeson warns, the "war on terrorism" is not "winnable" in the traditional sense; what is a pragmatic but moving target is the management and mitigation of Islamic extremist violence in a manner that it minimally interferes with daily life.[2]

This book continues ongoing research, whose initial theoretical foundations were first described in a scholarly monograph, *American Self-Radicalizing Terrorists and the Allure of "Jihadi Cool/Chic."*[3] Generally sketched, an understanding of how a culture of jihadi cool/chic self-propagates, principally on the internet, flows from the following premises. The internet provides the means through which a "self-activating terrorist" may first self-radicalize through some imaginary or sympathetic connection with an organized terrorist network. Additionally, the internet allows such a self-activating terrorist to move into the stage of radical violent action. The internet serves both functions by not only providing a potential self-radicalizing terrorist with a rhetorical medium for self-justification and communication through the use of "monster talk"[4] and its converse, the rhetoric about the "good citizen" but also by serving as a source for relatively inexpensive and more unpredictable technologies of mass destruction.

Crucial to this analysis is the distinction between a radicalization of thought and a radicalization of action. This is because a theoretical rhetoric of radicalization does not automatically convert into a rhetoric of radical action unless there are catalysts at work. The internet, as well as *imagined relations* cemented by the rhetorics of "jihadi cool" or "jihadi chic," along with a host of other factors, may function as these crucial catalysts, galvanizing monster talk into monstrous action. What differentiates this book from *American Self-Radicalizing Terrorists*[5] is that the prior manuscript focused specifically on a detailed case analysis of three well-known American self-activating terrorists: Colleen LaRose, Tamerlan Tsarnaev, and Dzokhar (Jahar) Tsarnaev. Each case study was mapped in a manner so as to describe key elements of each terrorist's childhood and early formative experiences, education, psychological factors, ideology, the turning point at which ideological commitment dictated that radical rhetoric be converted into radical action, and very briefly, the denouement thereafter. In contrast, in this book, the focus is on comparatively more recent and discrete global efforts to respond to the mystique of jihadi cool/chic within a US court and within mainstream culture, and internationally, which I describe in greater detail in the chapters that follow.

Using a more analytic and applied angle, this book focuses on *narrative patterns* that emerge from a sustained analysis of various myths regarding terrorism and counter-terrorism. Indeed, the power of narrative in relation to understanding propagating terrorism and producing effective counter-terrorism rhetorical strategies has long been recognized by both governmental and nongovernmental entities. In 2009, the Office of Naval Research (ONR) funded a research project, "Identifying and Countering Extremist Narratives," aimed at identifying and analyzing the "master narratives" that characterize Islamist extremist narratives; the study was spearheaded by Communications scholars at the University of Arizona.[6] In 2012, the Pentagon's Defense Advanced Research Projects Agency (DARPA) funded a concept, "narrative networks," targeted at studying the connections between narrative and neuroscience with the goal of enhancing national security by understanding the neurobiology of what persuades people to move into radical action. As described by William Casebeer, the lead DARPA official for this project, "neural networks" aimed to "understand how narratives influence human thoughts and behavior, then apply those findings to a security context in order to address security challenges such as radicalization, violent social mobilization, insurgency and terrorism, and conflict prevention and resolution."[7] Similarly, the Rand Corporation's 2011 presentation on "Strategic Narratives: Their Uses and Limitations" to the US Advisory Commission on Public Diplomacy made policy recommendations regarding the ownership, guidance, and control of narratives, and the management of narrative conflict, with a particular, but not exclusive, focus on the deployment of mass media, within a security context.[8] Within this context, one goal of this research program is not to come up with a competing master narrative. This is because to attempt to do so would only *reinscribe or reinforce* the pattern of rigid ideological rhetorical warfare from which this project attempts to break. Rather, this book aims to locate arious fissures and gaps that reside within global terrorist master narratives;

to uncover strategically concealed alternative possibilities hidden within these master narratives' seemingly seamless contours; and to unveil logical fallacies, unverifiable presuppositions, and absolutist moral prescriptions masked as neutral descriptions. This research program also analyzes the dynamics of recent examples of counter-terrorist rhetorical strategies and qualitatively assesses their effectiveness as counter- or alternative narratives. Thus, generally speaking, this book aims to present numerous contributions to different fields (while maintaining complex and porous disciplinary boundaries) and ongoing debates in ethics and the philosophy of law.

Chapter 1, "The Rhetoric and Aesthetic of 'Jihadi Cool/Chic,'" is principally an explanation for the scope of this book. Briefly outlined, this work builds upon a research program that explains the power or allure of jihadi cool/chic.[9] Thus, it begins with a description of what that culture of jihadi cool/chic is.[10] Nevertheless, what is new is the analysis of more recent instances, in the United States (and globally), of counter-terrorist narratives that emerge from concrete legal and media examples within the context of a "poethics" of witnessing to the trauma and horror embedded within jihadi cool/chic accounts.

Chapter 2 is titled "*Raza v. New York*: An Attempt at a Counter-Narrative with Mixed Results." One of the implicit claims in jihadi cool/chic media, as specifically espoused by ISIS, for instance, is that "real" Muslims, ethically moved by the suffering of Muslims worldwide, must join the global war by becoming warriors of the Caliphate. One corollary, equally as fallacious, which unconsciously mimes jihadi cool's claim, and has dangerously shaped much law enforcement and public policy in relation to radicalization, is that practicing Islam is the necessary gateway to radicalization, leading to a particularly linear and reductive model of how radicalization occurs, initially formulated and put into practice by the New York Police Department (NYPD). The legal and popular ramifications that flow from this assumption are analyzed in this section.

Chapter 3 is titled "Countering Jihadi Chic: The Myth of the Jihadi Bride and the Yazidi Genocide." One of the implicit claims in jihadi cool/chic media is that becoming a jihadi bride is liberating and humanizing. This romanticized myth is undercut by the realities of the atrocities committed by ISIS, its fighters, and their families against the Yazidis, especially females, whom they considered irredeemably "dirty infidels." This chapter analyzes ISIS's religious jurisprudence in relation to other faiths, with a special emphasis on the Yazidi faith, which ISIS singled out for destruction based on "scholarly" analyses. The chapter closes by engaging in a legal analysis that shows that ISIS committed genocide, crimes against humanity, and war crimes against the Yazidis using an organized and thorough-going system of extermination, rape, torture, forcible transfer, sexual enslavement, enslavement, and indoctrination of Yazidis simply because they were Yazidi.

Chapter 4, the most deeply philosophical and theoretical of the chapters, summarizes the book's findings and indicates other potential areas for further research, such as in the examination of the conditions of possibility within which a "poethics" of witnessing may be explored. Drawing from Levinasian and Kantian ethics, this chapter engages the responsibility of the reader in bearing witness to the traumatic phenomena that the book analyzes.

The Rhetoric and Aesthetic of "Jihadi Cool/Chic"[11]

The Genesis and Evolution of "Jihadi Cool"

The terms "jihadi cool" or "jihadi chic" have been much used in the media, especially with the beheading of American photojournalist James Foley in 2014 by "Jihadi John," identified by the British MI5 to be former London rapper Abdel-Majed Abdel Bary.[12] Mumbai-born British author Salman Rushdie expressed fears that the language of "jihadi cool," propagated through Twitter and YouTube, was seducing young British Muslims to join the "decapitating barbarism"[13] of ISIS (an acronym for "Islamic State in Iraq Syria," also alternatively termed "Islamic State in the Levant" or "Islamic State in al Sham").[14] Rushdie defined "jihadi cool" as "the deformed medievalist language of fanaticism, backed up by modern weaponry," and opined that "[i] t's hard not to conclude that this hate-filled religious rhetoric, pouring from the mouths of ruthless fanatics into the ears of angry young men, has become the most dangerous new weapon in the world today."[15] In a similar vein, House Homeland Security Committee Chairman Mike McCaul (R-Texas) raised concerns about the sufficiency of the Obama administration's response to emergent threats from "the 'jihadi cool' subculture—young individuals influenced by the sophisticated propaganda campaigns of Muslim extremist groups such as the Islamic State and Al-Qaeda in the Arabian Peninsula."[16] Similarly, Major General Michael K. Nagata focused on the Islamic State's "magnetic attraction" as a key to understanding, and to destabilizing, its rhetorical campaign online; he stated: "I want to engage in a long-term conversation to understand a commonly held view of the psychological, emotional and cultural power of I.S. [Islamic State] in terms of a diversity of audiences. . . . They are drawing people to them in droves. There are I.S. T-shirts and mugs."[17]

The term "jihadi cool" was originally coined by psychiatrist and former Central Intelligence Agency (CIA) operations officer, Marc Sageman, to describe Al-Qaeda's growing influence on the internet.[18] Despite the prevalence of monstrous metaphors pointing to an utterly foreign menace infecting or seducing American or British men, the concept of "jihadi cool" probably began with Adam Yahiye Gadahn, an American raised on a goat farm in Riverside County, who spent some of his teenage years with his Jewish grandfather in Santa Ana.[19] Gadahn left for Pakistan in the 1990s and emerged around 2004 on propaganda videos as an English-speaking spokesman for Al-Qaeda.[20] Although Gadahn's early videos as "Azzam the American" were viewed as more "laughable" than "scary," these rough productions were nevertheless noted as among the first English-language radical jihadist propaganda efforts attempting to reach out to Western audiences.[21]

Additionally, the slick website of Revolution Muslim became a precursor of what has evolved into the look of "jihadi cool." Over an eighteen-month period, this small New York-based organization peaked until government officials arrested one of its leaders and shut down the website.[22] Revolution Muslim was created by three American converts to radical Islam, all of whom are serving prison sentences.[23] At the height of its popularity, the website was used by authorities to monitor the communication, recruitment, and activities of aspiring radical jihadis.[24]

With the shutdown of the Revolution Muslim website, *Inspire* magazine, an online publication run by the group Al-Qaeda in the Arabian Peninsula targeting English-language speakers, moved in to fill the gap.[25] Described as akin to "the *Sports Illustrated* of jihad," this magazine published articles such as one giving instructions on creating explosive devices, a copy of which was found in the backpack of one of the Tsarnaev brothers.[26]

One of *Inspire* magazine's productions, the *Lone Mujahid Pocketbook*, produced in Spring 2013, advertised itself as "A Step to [*sic*] Step Guide on How to Become a Successful Lone Mujahid."[27] The issue clearly targeted would-be American jihadis and employed hip, fashionable language conventions as well as rap lingo to tantalize and inundate its audience with tips, strategies, and incitement to commit acts of terrorism. For example, the cover of that issue drew in its potential readers with the lines:

> R U dreamin' of wagin' jihadi attacks against kuffar? . . . Well, there's no need to travel abroad, coz the frontline has come to you. Wanna know how? Just read "n" apply the contents of this guide which had [*sic*] practical "n" creative ways to please Allah by killing his enemies "n" healing the believers' chests.[28]

The contents reprised many of *Inspire's* first ten issues, such as "Make a Bomb in the Kitchen of your Mom" and the "Ultimate Mowing Machine."[29] Deploying everyday items such as sugar, motor oil, or pressure cookers, and systematically detailing tactical details such as different types of bombs, areas most vulnerable to a mass attack, and methods of maximizing mayhem, the issue sought to convert its everyday audiences into radical jihadi warriors. "Mixing religious devotion with a desire to be cool in the MTV generation, the magazine offer[ed] an attractive picture for jihadi wannabes, perhaps inspired by the mass popular appeal of rapping gang-bangers who ma[de] gun violence 'cool.'"[30]

Yet even *Inspire*'s glossy and sophisticated manipulation of the media was eclipsed by ISIS's deft deployment of social media, such as Twitter and Facebook, which showcased items as diverse as graphic videos to T-shirts[31] featuring ISIS's logo, which is a black flag.[32] Former Director of the National Counterterrorism Center Michael Leiter acknowledged that ISIS "is using more social media than [A]l[-]Qaeda ever did."[33] Similarly, according to Staffan Truve, an analyst with Recorded Future, a nongovernment entity that monitors Twitter and other social media, in summer 2014 alone, more than 60,000 internet accounts expressed positive sentiments regarding ISIS extremists.[34] An even larger number can be extrapolated by multiplying that figure by an average account's tweets, combined with the group's deft use of other social media, inclusive of the Android app; Truve estimates that "hundreds of thousands of people are receiving the Islamic State message."[35] The imagery Truve uses, in describing ISIS's carefully tailored global recruitment campaign, is reminiscent of a mythological hydra—cut one head off, and another blooms to rear its deadly head: "Every time a pro-IS Twitter account is closed, another one almost immediately takes its place."[36] Furthermore, ISIS has taken "jihadi cool" to new merchandising extremes: it now features its own online clothing line run by a company, Zirah Moslem, which specializes in ISIS-themed T-shirts and hoodies, sold via websites in Indonesia, where it is legal to sell jihadi-themed products.[37]

Finally, in February 2023, an Iranian foundation praised Hadi Matar, the 24-year-old Shi'ite Muslim American who, after coming back from a trip to Lebanon, allegedly viciously stabbed Salman Rushdie in the face, neck, and body during a literary event at the Chautauqua Institution in New York.[38] Mohammad Esmail Zarei, secretary of the Foundation to Implement Imam Khomeini's Fatwas, stated:

> We sincerely thank the brave action of the young American who made Muslims happy by blinding one of Rushdie's eyes and disabling one of his hands. Rushdie is now no more than living dead and, to honour this brave action, about 1,000 square metres of agricultural land will be donated to the person or any of his legal representatives.[39]

Although Matar was silent on whether he was inspired by Ayatollah Ruhollah Khomeini's 1989 fatwa calling for the deaths of anyone associated with the publication of Rushdie's book, *The Satanic Verses*, there are indirect indications that Matar was probably inspired by Khomeini.[40] He guardedly stated: "I respect the ayatollah. I think he's a great person. That's as far as I will say about that."[41] In comparison, regarding Rushdie, all Matar stated was that because Rushdie had attacked Islam, he did not like him very much.[42] Matar denied contact with Iran's Revolutionary Guard,[43] though it is clear that he came back a changed man after a trip to Lebanon where his father allegedly refused to see him.[44] Regardless of the lack of clear connections to Iran, the foundation continued to praise Matar and went as far as stating that the same amount of farmland—1,000 square meters—would be given to anyone who would eventually succeed at taking Rushdie's life, showing that the fatwa's rhetorical force remains a potent lure.[45]

Explaining the Seductive Appeal of "Jihadi Cool"

How does one explain this upsurge of "jihadi cool" popularity? One factor appears to be the seductive appeal of being a "badass." As the University of California-Los Angeles sociologist Jack Katz noted: "In many youthful circles, to be 'bad,' to be a 'badass' or otherwise overtly embrace symbols of deviance is regarded as a good thing."[46] Katz identifies three stages of aggression that a badass aspirant must undergo and become in order to become initiated into the ranks of the truly "badass." First, he must be tough and morally impermeable—not someone who can easily be influenced by others. Second, he must appear alien—uncompromisingly "hostile to any form of civilization" and irreducible to anything comprehensible to "native sensibilities," resulting in his presence or acts as "unnerving."[47] Third, and ultimately, to be a "badass" requires a genuine meanness, or the spontaneous ability to engage in acts of violence, devoid of considerations of either utility or self-preservation; "badasses manifest the transcendent superiority of their being, specifically by insisting on the dominance of their will . . . ."[48]

Perhaps the seduction of "jihadi cool" is simply the paradigmatic appeal of the "badass" given a jihadi mask. As Simon Cottee observes:

> The paradigmatic badass is still with us, only now he doesn't have a gangster face; now he has a jihadi face. For the ultimate badasses are the caliphate-invoking, kafir-hating, sword-wielding men in black of Islamic State. This is in no way to glamorize the group. But it may be the key to understanding why some young men from the West give up everything to join it or affiliated groups.[49]

However, a second, and, to some extent, contrary explanation is the success of promoting a romanticized notion of making one's mark on the world through adventure, linked with a promise of earthly pleasure—to which allure the badass is theoretically immune, with his imperviousness, toughness, and meanness. This notion, the idea of a "five star jihad," appears to have two components: (1) the allure of celebrity, and (2) the attractions of living in luxury while being "virtuous." Lorne Dawson, a University of Waterloo sociologist, theorized that "our celebrity-obsessed culture pushes youth to define who they are at ever earlier stages. There is this burden on kids to recreate or reinscribe themselves in their own narratives. They're trying to figure out 'how can I be special?'"[50] This image of celebrity comes with stereotypes of necessary luxury. Hence, internet images aimed to recruit UK-born Islamic warriors showcased jihadis "lounging in a well-appointed home with laptops and game systems."[51] For example, reading a Tumblr account of what young British jihadis can enjoy once they penetrate Syria's borders (through a bribe), gives one the impression that they have achieved the (masculine) earthly version of paradise; not only do they enjoy houses with "5+ bedrooms with swimming pools, *etc.*" but also "junk food and sweets, training with a wide range of weapons, internet, phones, cheeseburgers lol [*sic*] pizza [not 'foreign muck like tabbouleh or hummus'], kebabs, markets, schools for children, classes for adults, shariah courts . . . ."[52] And if weapons, food, and Brotherhood are not enough, calls for fresh recruits throw in additional tantalizing hooks: "There are plenty of women here waiting to be married; waiting to bare [*sic*] the offspring of the army of Imam Mehdi by the will of Allah and there is honour for the Muslims here."[53]

There are numerous accounts of young jihadi warriors posting "selfies" of themselves glamorously atop tanks and brandishing guns or showing some heartwarmingly human aspect. One such internet celebrity was a Dutch national of Turkish descent, who engaged in the armed struggle against the Syrian regime, called Yilmaz.[54] After the photo-sharing site Instagram closed his site, Yilmaz migrated to Tumblr, a blogging platform favored by jihadi warriors eager to boast of their feats in battle.[55] Some of Yilmaz's popular photos included one of himself tenderly cradling a Syrian toddler swathed in pink, and another of himself, immortalized in the quintessential warrior pose, dressed in a black jacket and camouflage, with one leg propped up and his rifle by his side.[56] Yilmaz's self-promotion paid off: not only did he develop a following among Syria watchers but he also achieved a presence in international news when the *New York Times* blogged about him.[57] Like other Hollywood celebrities, he used social media to make sure his fan base remained secure; he deployed the ask-and-answer forum platform of Ask.fm to answer fan questions about his grand adventure.[58] Hardly surprisingly, his success spawned imitators—"Other jihadis emulated him, posting photos of themselves on Facebook, Twitter, and other platforms looking happy and relaxed, pointing fingers in the air and casually slinging guns or other weapons."[59] The ripple effects were clear, pointing to the power of jihadi cool. In an interview with Dutch TV show *Nieuwsuur* in 2014, where Yilmaz was shown leading new recruits in target practice in a bleak Syrian field, Yilmaz opined that "90 percent of [the recruits had] never even fired a bullet in their lives, let alone [fought] on an actual battlefield."[60]

Analyzing the Rhetorical Mechanics of "Jihadi Cool"

Very clearly, part of the reason why the "jihadi cool" message is so popular among particularly young men is its careful tailoring and understanding of its targeted audiences. A CIA report stated that approximately 2,000 Westerners had joined the ranks of the radical jihadi fighters in Iraq and Syria, with at least 500 from the United Kingdom and more than 700 from France.[61] Both the look and the content of "jihadi cool" were crafted principally by American radical jihadi converts Anwar al-Aulaqi, a New Mexico-born Muslim cleric based in Yemen; Omar Hammami, an Alabama native who rose to become a senior commander in Somalia and starred in a rap recruiting video, which became an internet sensation, in which Hammami led an armed group of fighters to a catchy musical beat; and Adam Gadahn, a native Californian who became an Al-Qaeda spokesman and was charged with treason in 2006, among others.[62] "Can you imagine [Ayman al-] Zawahiri or [Osama] bin Laden doing a rap video? That is something that people without the same connection to America or the West would have a harder time pulling off," proclaimed David Kris, Assistant Attorney General for National Security.[63]

Both the ability to communicate in the American vernacular in a manner that appeals to the youth, as well as a command of what it takes to create an MTV aesthetic (designed to sell music), are crucial components of jihadi cool's rhetorical persuasiveness. Videos created specifically for Western audiences try to depict jihad as a "Hollywood-like video game."[64] Quoting Patrick Skinner with the Soufan Group, a security intelligence services company:

> They make jihad seem cool, not over the top—beheading videos aren't recruitment videos—but they do do very slick productions, with music overlaid on top of very slick graphics, and they make it seem like a video game. They don't show the after effects. They'll show an attack or they'll show a killing, or they'll show shooting with explosions, and it's very Hollywood-like.[65]

Yet despite this imagined appeal to the virtual worlds of Hollywood video and MTV aesthetics, these "jihadi cool" videos attempt a connection to "reality" by humanizing the radical jihadi warriors. Hence, radical jihadi warriors are shown with cats and dogs,[66] and with American products that would appeal to their young audiences, such as Nutella, a chocolate spread, and Skittles, a rainbow-like colorful candy.[67] The British citizen suspected of being ISIS's sword in the beheading of James Foley in 2014, Abdel-Majed Abdel Bary, not only aspired to be a rapper, using curses for lyrics against a Western soundtrack, but also, in collaboration with his fellow British kidnappers, called themselves "The Beatles."[68] One of the radical jihadi "Beatles," Abu Abdullah al-Britani, expressed his passion for Krispy Kreme doughnuts on Twitter, while another radical jihadist in Syria posted a photo of himself drinking Red Bull.[69]

The crossover between the realms of the imagined and the real (as culturally imagined and rhetorically produced) can be quite startling and can sometimes border on the hyperbolic and humorous. For example, Ryan Mauro noted: "Another Islamic State's supporter's photo has a Batman-like image with an Islamic State flag on his costume. He recently tweeted that the Islamic State could defeat the Justice League, a team of comic-book superheroes including Batman and Superman."[70]

Thus, while appealing to the visual allure of the imagined realms of MTV and Hollywood video, in order to be convincing, the aesthetic of the "real" must also coexist with the realm of the virtual (a feature of monster talk and its counterpart, the discourse of the good citizen). Both, however, are culturally imagined and projected. The irony of jihadi cool/chic is that it deploys Western rhetorical tools to destroy the very culture that created these derivative rhetorical forms and culture, and it continues to buttress jihadi cool/chic with powerful persuasive appeal.

Phrased slightly differently, jihadi cool's rhetorical power lies in a simple formula hyperbolically magnified upon the collectively imagined stages of social media and the internet; to quote Christopher Dickey, a foreign editor of the *Daily Beast*, the formula that explains the power of jihadi cool is: "'TNT', which stands for Testosterone, Narrative and Theater."[71] As Elizabeth Pearson observed regarding what she termed "Grand Theft Auto Culture": "Being a 'Jihadi' is not just about ideology; it's about status, as a man. Increasingly, a nexus is being recognized between the macho masculinity of British street culture and criminal gangs, and the behaviours associated with pathways to violent extremism . . . ."[72] Interestingly, many of the radical jihadi converts were initially neither overtly religious nor openly political; many of them seemed "normal" to the point of being banal. But the rhetorical elements of jihadi cool seemed an irresistible siren's song. "Rap videos, romanticized notions of revolution and adventure; and first-hand accounts of the 'fun' of guerilla war . . . are the latest tactics used by militant recruiters as part of what experts have identified as an 'intensification or radicalization' both in the United States and elsewhere."[73]

Jihadi Cool and Gender

Prior sections make clear the intimate connection between jihadi cool and the performance of masculinity. What of femininity, as it is clear that not only men but also women are subject to jihadi cool's/chic's allure? *Inspire* magazine, which is geared toward a male audience has a female counterpart: *Al-Shamikha* magazine, which features articles like "Interview with a Jihadi Wife" and "Facing Destruction: Steps to Alleviate Your Pain and Ways to Reach a Cleaner and Better Path."[74] The first article claims to be an "exclusive" interview with a jihadi wife praising her husband's martyrdom and dispensing an essential tip for living virtuously: "When walking, do not look left or right to avoid attracting sin."[75] Magnus Ranstorp, Research Director at the Center for Asymmetric Threat Studies at the Swedish National Defense College, remarked: "By catering to women, Al-Qaeda publications are underlining the operational role women play (in terrorist attacks), which is largely ignored, as well as their cultural role in this specific society."[76]

More recently, ISIS as well has pitched its recruitment toward young women, but principally as jihadi brides and mothers. For example, one such overt recruitment enticed women to join ISIS in the following way:

> You may wear your veils without being harassed, no woman is harmed here and if she is there is a harsh penalty as the woman's honour is not tampered with whatsoever, there are plenty of mujahideen desiring to get married who have some of the most loving and softest characters I have ever witnessed even though they are lions in the battlefield, there are orphans here waiting for mothers to love them the way their parents would have. Come to the land of honour. You are needed here.[77]

The recruitment tactics are also working on women, producing a surge in what has been called "jihadi girl power subculture," as "hundreds" of Western Muslim women have traveled to Syria to marry radical jihadi warriors, sending out a flood of messages via the internet.[78] That Western women, with all their freedoms, choose instead a more traditional lifestyle is a huge morale boost for the radical jihadi troops, argues Sasha Havicek, director of the London-based Institute for Strategic Dialogue.[79] Like the young men who convert, the young women are also young (in general, the demographic covers ages 15–22), and are also well versed in the use of social media such as Twitter, Tumblr, and Kik.[80] And although they may pine nostalgically for some imagined version of the lifestyle of early Muslims, the language they use is extremely contemporary, replete with tech-savvy slang and emoticons, with a dash of Arabic religious terms spelled out in English letters—to flash their credentials as being "part of the gang."

Of course, there is intelligence that indicates contrary results. Federal investigators believe that approximately one hundred Americans, including women, have traveled to Syria to join radical jihadi groups, though this number is not certain.[81] According to these reports, some women are seduced into joining by the lure of becoming virtual Florence Nightingale, as nurses

IJ

and medical assistants.[82] However, once they do join, they become virtual sex slaves[83]—much like Jamie Paulin Ramirez.

And though these women converts profess to be innocuous, posing no threat to national security, in their online posts, amid the overwhelmingly domestic and apolitical tweets about washing and the beauty of the sky, are nuggets about the bravery of radical jihadi warriors, who are "real men," unlike the enemy troops—the Kafir (infidels).[84] For example, Muhajirah Amatullah wrote regarding the ISIS warriors: "Thy [*sic*] sleep w/eyes open + chop heads off."[85] Even more radically, Umm Hussain al-Britani, whom the British press identified as a forty-five-year-old Muslim convert Sally Jones, a one-time singer in a band, stated in her October Twitter feed that "taking female Kafirs [unbelievers] as slaves is ibadah [an act of worship]."[86] Startlingly, it appears to be the women who prove to be staunch defenders of strict moral codes; a Twitter account, identifying itself by the handle "@irhabbyukhts" or "terrorist sisters" (an apparent attempt at irony), dedicates itself to the mission of naming and shaming jihadi men who flirt online with girls.[87]

Notwithstanding the similarities between the rhetorical appeals made to young Western men and women to convert, there is a strict gender demarcation that seems predominantly in place: the place of honor, for a man, is on the battlefield; for a woman, it is the home. (Virtuous) men fight and slaughter the enemy mercilessly; (good) women bear children, tend to domestic chores, and praise their men's feats on the battlefield. That distinction, as pointed out in the case of Colleen LaRose, was not as clear; she was neither young, of ideal childbearing age (in fact, she was incapable of bearing children), nor technologically savvy. She did not shy away from flirting with Muslim men online, and in fact, actively sought it. Nevertheless, the allure of jihadi cool clearly worked its magic on Colleen LaRose in her conversion.[88]

Thus, this chapter reconstructed with precision the aestheticization of violence embodied in the phenomenon of jihadi cool/chic. This amounted to a virtual campaign tailored to the dominant codes of social networks in liberal societies. Of particular emphasis was the detail pertaining to the construction of gender roles and how the humanization of jihadis is achieved through various visual techniques and representations that draw from the visual culture of social media. This initial analysis is a crucial building block to the book's final chapter, which connects what may appear as disparate issues and seeks to articulate the act of witnessing from an ethical perspective.

Notes

1 See, for example, Angel Rabasa, Stacie L. Pettyjohn, Jeremy J. Ghez, and Christopher Boucek, *Deradicalizing Islamist Extremists*, Rand Corporation (Arlington, Virginia: National Security Research Division, 2010), accessed October 13, 2016, https://www.ojp.gov/ncjrs/virtual-library/abstracts/deradicalizing-islamist-extremists.

2 See generally, Greg C. Reeson, *Why We Can't Win the War on Terror and What We Should Do Instead* (Lanham, MD: Government Institutes, 2011).

3 Caroline Joan "Kay" S. Picart, *American Self-Radicalizing Terrorists and the Allure of "Jihadi Cool/Chic"* (Newcastle upon Tyne: Cambridge Scholars Publishing, 2017).

4 The term "monster talk" is grounded in a theoretical framework, Gothic Criminology, which I developed in collaboration with Cecil Greek, a sociologist. Noting the proliferation of monstrous metaphors not only in popular culture but also in academic and public policy discourses, this framework attempts to track the complex connections binding the "real" and the "reel" in mediated discourses and narratives. For an example of how this can be applied to the capture, trial, and sentencing of the New York/New Jersey bomber, see Caroline Joan "Kay" S. Picart, "Monstrous Discourses, Jihadi Cool, and Emergent Counter-Terrorist Narratives: The Case of Ahmad Khan Rahami (a.k.a. Ahmad Rahimi) and the 2016 New York/New Jersey Bombings," in *Monsters, Law, Crime: Exploration in Gothic Criminology* (Madison, NJ: Fairleigh Dickinson University Press, 2021), 245–80.

5 See generally, Picart, *American Self-Radicalizing Terrorists*..

6 Jeffry R. Halverson, H.L. Goodall, Jr., and Steven R. Corman, *Master Narratives of Islamist Extremism* (London: Palgrave Macmillan, 2011), ix.

7 J.D. Heyes, "Pentagon Researching 'Narrative Networks' as Way to Hijack the Brain with False Stories," *Natural News*, May 15, 2012, https://www.naturalnews.com/035872_Pentagon_narrative_networks_propaganda.html.

8 Eric V. Larson, "Strategic Narratives: Their Uses and Limitations" (PowerPoint presentation, US Advisory Commission on Public Diplomacy),

Rand Corporation, November 29, 2011, https://www.state.gov/documents/organization/180021.pdf.

9 Picart, *American Self-Radicalizing Terrorists.*

10 For a parallel analysis, see Orit Kamir's description of an "honor"-based culture as opposed to one based on "dignity." Orit Kamir, *Betraying Dignity: The Toxic Seduction of Social Media, Shaming, and Radicalization* (Lanham, MD: Fairleigh Dickinson University Press, 2020).

11 This section is adapted, with permission, from Picart, *American Self-Radicalizing Terrorists*, at 17–26. The author thanks Cambridge Scholars Publishing.

12 Stephen Z. Nemo, "Jihadi Cool: Hip Hop Earns its Bad Rap," *Communities Digital News*, August 26, 2014, http://www.commdiginews.com/politics-2/commentary/jihadi-cool-hip-hop-earns-its-bad-rap-24622/.

13 Salman Rushdie, "'Jihadi Cool' Language Luring Britons to Islamic State," *Haaretz,* October 11, 2014, http://www.haaretz.com/news/middle-east/1.620223.

14 Rushdie, who migrated to New York, was the subject of a fatwa from Ayatollah Khomeini in 1989 for his novel, *The Satanic Verses* (1988), and had to spend years in hiding. "'Jihadi-Cool' Language Luring Young British Muslims to Islamic State, Salman Rushdie Says," *Times of India*, October 12, 2014, http://timesofindia.indiatimes.com/world/uk/Jihadi-cool-language-luring-young-British-Muslims-to-Islamic-State-Salman-Rushdie-says/articleshow/44791862.cms.

15 Jerry Coyne, "Salman Rushdie Condemns 'Jihadi Cool'," *Why Evolution Is True*, October 12, 2014, 6:32 AM, http://whyevolutionistrue.wordpress.com/2014/10/12/salman-rushdie-condemns-jihadi-cool/.

16 Josh Hicks, "Rep. McCaul Questions U.S. Response to 'Jihadi Cool' Threat," *Washington Post*, September 12, 2014, http://www.washingtonpost.com/blogs/federal-eye/wp/2014/09/12/rep-mccaul-questions-u-s-response-to-jihadi-cool-threat/; Michael McCaul, "Islamic State Is Recruiting America's 'Jihadi Cool' Crowd," *Wall Street Journal*, September 11, 2014, 7:37 PM, http://www.wsj.com/articles/michael-mccall-islamic-state-is-recruiting-americas-jihadi-cool-crowd-1410478638.

17 Eric Schmitt, "In Battle to Defang ISIS, U.S. Targets Its Psychology," *New York Times*, December 28, 2014, http://www.nytimes.com/2014/12/29/us/politics/in-battle-to-defang-isis-us-targets-its-psychology-.html?_r=0.

18 Allen Benjamin Jones, "Jihadi Cool," *Not Theology Blog*, July 24, 2013, http://nottheology.com/2013/07/24/jihadi-cool-2/.

19 Theresa Walker, "Has ISIS Reached O.C.? Arrest Here Intensifies Questions," *Orange County Register*, August 30, 2014, 5:05 PM, http://www.ocregister.com/articles/dandach-633351-isis-orange.html.
20 Ibid.
21 Ibid.
22 Ibid.
23 Ibid.
24 Ibid.
25 IPT News, "Jihad is Cool: Jihadist Magazines Recruit Young Terrorists," *Investigative Project on Terrorism*, April 11, 2013, 4:39 PM, http://www.investigativeproject.org/3969/jihad-is-cool-jihadist-magazines-recruit-young.
26 Walker, "Has ISIS Reached O.C.?"
27 IPT News, "Jihad is Cool."
28 Ibid.
29 Ibid.
30 Ibid.; Steven Emerson, "Jihadists Magazines Recruit Young Terrorists," *Algemeiner*, April 15, 2013, 1:09 AM, http://www.algemeiner.com/2013/04/15/jihadist-magazines-recruit-young-terrorists/.
31 Morgan Brittany, "'Jihad Cool'—Recruiting Terrorists from America," *World Net Daily*, September 26, 2014, 7:53 PM, http://www.wnd.com/2014/08/jihad-cool-recruiting-terrorists-from-america/.
32 Walker, "Has ISIS Reached O.C.?"
33 Melanie Hunter, "Former Counterterror Official: 'We Don't Have Enough Muslim FBI Agents,'" *CNS News*, October 27, 2014, http://www.cnsnews.com/news/article/melanie-hunter/former-counterterror-official-we-dont-have-enough-muslim-fbi-agents.
34 Sharon Behn, "ISIS Militants Use 'Jihadi Cool' to Recruit Globally," *VOA News*, September 5, 2014, 5:39 PM, http://www.voanews.com/content/isis-militants-use-jihadi-cool-to-recruit-globally/2440430.html.
35 Ibid.
36 Ibid.
37 "The Jihad Shopping Network, Courtesy of ISIS," *Warrior*, June 24, 2014, accessed June 1, 2024, http://warrior.scout.com/story/1414293-the-jihad-shopping-network-courtesy-of-isis.
38 See "Iranian Foundation Praises Rushdie's Alleged Attacker, Offers Gift of Farmland," *RFE/RL's Radio Farda*, February 21, 2023, https://www.rferl.org/a/iran

-rushdie-attacker-land-gift/32281094.html; and Anders Hagstron, "Who is Hadi Matar? Everything We Need to Know About Salman Rushdie's Alleged Attacker," *FOXNews*, August 15, 2022, 10:08 AM, https://www.foxnews.com/us/hadi-matar-everything-we-know-salman-rushdies-alleged-attacker.

39 "Iranian Foundation Offers Land to Salman Rushdie's Attacker—State TV," *Reuters*, February 21, 2023, 5:18 AM, https://www.reuters.com/world/middle-east/iranian-foundation-offers-land-salman-rushdies-attacker-state-media-2023-02-21/.

40 Steven Vago and Ben Kesslen, "Salman Rushdie Attacker Praises Iran's Ayatollah, Surprised Author Survived: Jailhouse Interview," *New York Post*, August 17, 2022, 11:36 AM, https://nypost.com/2022/08/17/alleged-salman-rushdie-attacker-didnt-think-author-would-survive/.

41 Ibid.

42 Ibid.

43 Ibid.

44 Hagstron, "Who is Hadi Matar? Everything We Need to Know About Salman Rushdie's Alleged Attacker."

45 Vago and Kesslen, "Salman Rushdie."

46 Jack Katz, *Seductions of Crime: Moral and Sensual Attractions in Doing Evil* (New York: Basic Books, 1988), 80.

47 Ibid.

48 Ibid. at 81.

49 Simon Cottee, "Op-Ed: Islamic State's Badass Path to Paradise," *Los Angeles Times*, September 6, 2014, 5:00 AM, http://www.latimes.com/opinion/op-ed/la-oe-0907-cottee-badass-jihadi-cool-20140907-story.html#page=1.

50 Craig Kielburger and Marc Kielburger, "No Easy Answers to Terrorist Recruitment," *Exeter Lakeshore Times Advance*, October 10, 2014, http://www.lakeshoreadvance.com/2014/10/09/how-do-young-canadians-end-up-among-the-jihadis.

51 Ibid.

52 Aris Roussinos, "Jihad Selfies: These British Extremists in Syria Love Social Media," *Vice.com*, December 5, 2013, 8:40 AM, http://www.vice.com/read/syrian-jihadist-selfies-tell-us-a-lot-about-their-war.

53 Ibid.

54 Karen Leigh and Bruce Crumley, "New Jihadi Recruitment Tool: Militants' Instagram Accounts," *Christian Science Monitor*, June 10, 2014, http://www

.csmonitor.com/World/Middle-East/2014/0610/ New-jihadi-recruitment-tool-militants-Instagram-accounts.

55 Ibid.

56 Ibid.

57 Ibid.

58 Aryeh Savir, "ISIS Teen CRISIS: Jihadist Recruitment of American Kids," *United with Israel*, October 29, 2014, http://unitedwithisrael.org/isis-teen-crisis-jihadist-recruitment-of-american-kids/.

59 Leigh and Crumley, "New Jihadi Recruitment Tool."

60 Ibid.

61 Savir, "ISIS Teen CRISIS."

62 Spencer S. Hsu, "Arrest of Va. Man Spotlights Al-Qaeda's New American Recruiters," *Washington Post*, August 1, 2010, http://www.washingtonpost.com/wp-dyn/content/article/2010/07/31/AR 2010073102680.html?sid=ST2010072106133.

63 Ibid.

64 Behn, "ISIS Militants Use 'Jihadi Cool' to Recruit Globally."

65 Ibid.

66 Ryan Mauro, "ISIS: 'Cool' Image Winning Over Next Generation of Jihadis," *Clarion Project*, August 31, 2014, https://web.archive.org/web/20150720192107/http:/www.clarionproject.org/analysis/islamic-state-winning-over-next-generation-jihadis.

67 Behn, "ISIS Militants Use 'Jihadi Cool' to Recruit Globally."

68 Mauro, "ISIS: 'Cool' Image."

69 Ibid.

70 Ibid.

71 Savir, "ISIS Teen CRISIS."

72 Elizabeth Pearson, "Macho Cool: The Appeal of Violent Jihad," *Connect Justice Blog*, September 30, 2013, https://web.archive.org/web/20131001074900/http:/www.connectjustice.org/blog.php?d=3..

73 R.C. Porter, ""Jihad Cool"—Young Americans Lured to Fight for ISIS Militants; Seeds of Next 9/11?," *Fortuna's Corner*, June 28, 2014, https://web.archive.org/web/20180609070132/http:/fortunascorner.com/2014/06/28/jihad-cool-young-americans-lured-to-fight-for-isis-militants-seeds-of-next-911/.

74 Mona Alami, "Al-Qaeda Using Magazines to Spread Message," *USA Today*, April 20, 2011, http://usatoday30.usatoday.com/news/world/2011-04-19-al-qaeda-magazines.htm.

75 Ibid.

76 Ibid.

77 Roussinos, "Jihad Selfies."

78 Heba Saleh, "Western Female Jihadis Deploy 'Soft-Power' of Isis Online," *Financial Times*, October 28, 2014, http://www.ft.com/cms/s/0/2d8b020c-5792-11e4-8493-00144feab7de.html.

79 Ibid.

80 Ibid.

81 M.L. Ward, "Second American Jihadi Confirmed Dead in ISIS," *Uptown Magazine*, August 29, 2014, https://web.archive.org/web/20151024033701/https://www.uptownmagazine.com/2014/08/second-american-jihadi-confirmed-dead-isis/2/.

82 Ibid.

83 Ibid.

84 Saleh, "Western Female Jihadis Deploy."

85 Ibid.

86 Ibid.

87 Ibid.

88 See Picart, *American Self-Radicalizing Terrorists*, at 41–59.

2

Raza v. New York

An Attempt at a Counter-Narrative with Mixed Results

Radicalization Theory as a Fallacious Master Narrative

As explained in Chapter 1, one of the implicit claims in jihadi cool/chic media, as specifically espoused by ISIS, is that "real" Muslims, ethically moved by the suffering of Muslims worldwide, must join the global war by becoming warriors of the Caliphate. Phil Gursky succinctly distilled the potent content of the Al-Qaeda master narrative into three components:

(1) The West hates Islam and Muslims.
(2) The West is in a state of perpetual war with Islam and Muslims.
(3) True Muslims have a divine mandate to fight in a violent jihad.[1]

The master narrative thus positions Muslims as righteous victims, and therefore burdens the recipients of its message with an ethical imperative to avenge all alleged wrongs done to all Muslims by the monolithic "West."[2] Along a parallel track, this extremist master narrative is heavily espoused by Salafi-Jihadism, as distinct from Salafism and Jihadism. Salafis believe that the most authentic and truest version of Islam is recovered by a return to not only the spirit but also the letter of law, as lived by the early, righteous Muslims (Salafs), closest in time and proximity to the Prophet Muhammad; thus, Salafis emulate both the manner of dress and habits of the Prophet by, for example, cuffing their trousers at ankle-length or brushing their teeth with a *miswak* (a natural cleaning twig).[3] Beyond personal modes of dress and habits of hygiene,

Salafis generally prefer a "quietist" approach to politics, avoiding confrontation with state authorities, and instead preferring preaching, religious education, and when engaging in politics, advocating for specific *shariah*-based policies.[4]

Jihadism, in comparison, is spurred by the idea that religiously sanctioned warfare (jihad) is an individual obligation (*fard ʿayn*) rather than a collective obligation enacted by legitimate representatives of the Muslim community (*fard kifaya*), as it was traditionally grounded in a specific set of circumstances (citing specific Quranic verses dealing with violence and the use of force), rules of classical warfare, and the clerical determination of whether war was justified.[5] The jurisprudence of jihad, traditionally, had a specific context and was bound by rules concerning classical rules of warfare. However, adherents of global jihad contend that Muslim leaders are no longer legitimate representatives and thus do not have the authority to command justified violence.

Salafi-jihadism, as instantiated in the jihadi cool/chic rhetoric espoused by groups like Al-Qaida and ISIS, is a particular confluence of these two particular schools of thought that stresses the military exploits of the Salaf in order to imbue their own violent objectives with a seemingly immediate divine imperative. Salafi-jihadis thus have distanced themselves from the development of Islamic law for over twelve centuries and have selectively dipped into shariah law when it grants them a justification but choose to ignore the boundaries of the law when the law prescribes certain limits.[6] Unmoored from Islamic classical scholarly underpinnings and context-laden development, Salafi-jihadists engage in a type of exceptionalism, regarding their interpretation of Islam as the only true form of Islam; consequently, they justify their acts of violence against even fellow Muslims if these do not share their views on the basis of *takfir*, or the excommunication of fellow Muslims who are regarded as apostates.[7] It is thus clear that this pathologizing narrative is the rhetorical currency being used to incite self-radicalizing individuals to engage in acts of violence. Along a parallel track, Ajit Maan does a very detailed analysis of specific examples of such "pathologizing" narratives, exposing the unverifiable premises, fallacies, faulty analogies, "white spaces" (the Derridean underside that the master narrative conceals but which it requires in order to achieve its rhetorical power), and invisible slippage from description to prescription that lurk behind jihadi cool/chic's master narrative's seemingly irrefutable logical façade.[8]

Ironically, one corollary, equally as fallacious, which unconsciously accepts and mimes one of jihadi cool's/chic's central premises, and has shaped much law enforcement and public policy in relation to radicalization, especially in the United States, is that *practicing Islam is the necessary gateway to radicalization.* Indeed, Amna Akbar's critique of how radicalization theory's cardinal postulate that an increase in the outward signs of religiosity and politicization inevitably leads to an increased threat of terrorism remains a timely caveat.[9]

The uncritical acceptance of this particular postulate led to a particularly linear and reductive model of how radicalization occurs, initially formulated and put into practice by the New York Police Department. Two senior intelligence analysts in the New York City Police Department, Mitchell Silber and Arvin Bhatt, developed a four-stage model to conceptualize the transition from radical thought to radical action.[10] The model was developed from performing a comparative case analysis of homegrown terrorist plots planned and/or enacted by terrorists in countries as diverse as Spain, the Netherlands, the United Kingdom, Australia, and Canada,[11] and within the United States, in places as diverse as Portland, Oregon; Lackawanna, New York; and Northern Virginia.[12] This model became "widely understood and accepted as the model for understanding and informing training and strategies for law enforcement officials in dealing with cases of terrorism."[13]

Briefly outlined, Silber and Bhatt characterized the Radicalization Process in four stages:[14] (1) Pre-Radicalization, (2) Self-Identification, (3) Indoctrination, and (4) Jihadization.[15] The first stage is the Pre-Radicalization Phase, in which individuals live "ordinary" lives and usually have no criminal history. Then, something tragic acts as a catalyst, causing these individuals to become alienated or disassociated from general society. These traumatic, catalytic events could range from losing a job, undergoing a divorce, a tragic accident, or a death in the family, among others.[16]

Such traumatic events leave a void, which must be filled, either by seeking spiritual guidance, for example, or by integrating into a group. This finding of a new "home" constitutes the second stage, Self-Identification. Although the forging of such new identities or memberships can be sought out in new physical spaces such as in mosques or schools where radical imams preach, more often, the most typical venue these days is virtual, through the internet, where anonymity appears to provide a measure of security. Thus, self-radicalization occurs technically at this stage, when an individual begins to seek out jihadist websites, for the purpose of filling such a spiritual void through establishing imagined relations with a virtual community.

Nevertheless, it is usually interaction with members of a virtual community that cements stage three—Indoctrination.[17] Social media serves to create a loose virtual community of radical mentors and likeminded extremists, who provide resources, support, and communication, thus furthering the individual's conversion to radicalization, and strengthening imagined ties to this loose, virtual community. Indeed, a May 2008 report by the US Senate Committee on Homeland Security concluded that the internet "play(s) a critical role throughout the radicalization process" because it is the principal medium through which potential self-activating terrorists can discover radical jihadi propaganda, become converted, and become connected with "the global Islamist terrorist movement."[18]

Once the individual's indoctrination has moved from radical rhetoric to the rhetoric of radical action, the individual has reached stage four—Jihadization, in which self-radicalized terrorists "accept their individual duty to participate in jihad and self-designate themselves as holy warriors or mujahideen," actively planning, preparing for, and executing terrorist attacks.[19]

It is important to note that the New York Police Department members were not singular outliers in espousing the view that American Muslims serve as the necessary support base for the radicalized propagation of Al-Qaeda-inspired ideology, and that "religion [Islam] is assumed to lie at the heart of Islamist terrorism."[20] Police chiefs from California, Kansas, and New Jersey expressed similar views;[21] Senator Joseph Lieberman, former Chairman of the US Senate's Homeland Security and Governmental Affairs Committee,[22] and his then-counterpart in the US House, Representative Peter King, stated similar concerns about the potential for attacks by American Muslims and commenced a series of hearings to investigate the threat.[23] This view also appeared to have achieved some popular support, as evidenced in the controversy over plans to build an Islamic cultural center in downtown Manhattan and widespread protests against mosques within the United States.[24]

While I think Silber and Bhatt's model has some *rough heuristic* (*but not reductively predictive*) value, as pointed out in *American Self-Radicalizing Terrorists*, the problem was that the model was used as an unqualified "terror checklist,"[25] leading to the criminalization of anything related to the practice of Islam, which brings us to the specific topic of the next section.

Raza v. New York: Criminalizing the Practice of Islam

In the aftermath of the 9/11 attacks, the New York Police Department (NYPD) initiated an intense covert surveillance operation that focused on Muslims in New York City and beyond. Two Associated Press reporters, Adam Goldman and Matt Apuzzo, revealed extensive evidence that the New York Police Department engaged in a comprehensive religious-based surveillance and mapping program targeted specifically at Muslims within the United States.[26] "Rakers" (police officers dressed in civilian clothing)[27] and "mosque crawlers" (informants embedded in Muslim communities) were deployed anywhere Muslims congregated, including coffee shops or even their own homes, without any suspicion of wrongdoing.[28] All mosques were labeled "terrorist organizations,"[29] leading to the necessary corollary that every Muslim was necessarily a potential terrorist, and this rationale provided the justification for infiltrating specific religious organizations with sweeping and lengthy surveillance operations, even if the New York Police Department had never criminally charged a particular mosque or Islamic organization.

"Rakers" and "mosque crawlers," as part of this secret dragnet surveillance operation, eavesdropped on conversations in restaurants and cafes, cataloged memberships in mosques and student organizations, and even occasionally engaged in entrapment-style tactics, baiting people into making inflammatory remarks. The Muslim Surveillance Program thus had two components: (1) the investigation of Muslims under a human-mapping "Zone Assessment" or "Demographics" Units to generate a database of the locations where Muslims lived or worked, and (2) the investigation of Muslims in order to carefully monitor any speech or actions that could be viewed as "reactionary."[30]

The New York Police Department implemented this particular counter-radicalization program with the assistance of the Central Intelligence Agency (CIA), leading to a dozen mosques coming under the scope of "terrorism enterprise investigations" (TEI). Placing a mosque under a "TEI" label effectively meant that anyone attending the institution was a potential terror suspect and could be subject to unrestricted surveillance.[31] Initially, the New York Police Department's Muslim Surveillance Program was conducted, partially, with the assistance of a CIA operative who had very little oversight from any agency and whose assignment was very loosely defined.[32] Following an internal investigation by the CIA's Inspector General, the operative's assignment was terminated and replaced with a different intelligence officer under a more formal arrangement to work for the New York Police Department.[33]

Because the CIA is technically not allowed to collect domestic intelligence, the overall effect was to make "the wall between domestic and foreign operations . . . more porous"[34] and to transform the New York Police Department into something structurally and functionally resembling a domestic branch of the CIA. Hardly surprisingly, with assistance from the CIA, the New York Police Department's Muslim Surveillance Program expanded well beyond the jurisdictional boundaries of New York, and into New Jersey, Pennsylvania, and Massachusetts.[35] The New York Police Department meticulously matched Pakistani-American officers to infiltrate Pakistani neighborhoods, Palestinians were dispatched into Palestinian neighborhoods, and so on, in order to "rake some coals, looking for hot spots," leading to the term "rakers."[36]

The "unusual activity" on which the Demographics Unit was authorized to conduct surveillance included such innocuous activities as a beauty supply store selling chemicals that could be used to make bombs, or a *hawala*—that is, a broker who could transfer money globally with little documentation, or an ethnic bookstore selling "radical literature."[37] Thus, despite protests from the collaboration between the CIA and the New York Police Department that all intelligence gathered resulted from traditional leads, the report from Apuzzo and Goldman demonstrated that "even the most generic lead was used to justify surveillance of entire neighborhoods."[38] Interestingly, although many people of Syrian heritage were Jewish, Jews were excluded from being monitored; similarly, documents regarding the Egyptian community excluded the Coptic [Christian] Egyptian community.[39] This revealed, once again, the assumption that Islam was the gateway toward radicalization.

On June 18, 2013, New York residents who were religious and community leaders, represented by the New York Civil Liberties Union (NYCLU), the American Civil Liberties Union (ACLU), and the Creating Law Enforcement Accountability and Responsibility (CLEAR) project of Main Street Legal Services, Inc. at the City University of New York School of Law, filed a lawsuit in the US District Court for the Eastern District of New York. The lawsuit, *Raza v. City of New York*,[40] argued that the New York Police Department's Muslim Surveillance Program violated the Fourteenth Amendment's Equal Protection Clause, the First Amendment's right to the free exercise of religion and the guarantee of neutrality to all religions, and the New York State Constitution. Another lawsuit, *Handschu v. Police Dep't*,[41] regarding the widespread religious profiling of Muslim New Yorkers, was similarly filed by the ACLU in 2012.[42]

In January 2016, the New York Police Department settled both cases. As a result of these negotiations, there were modified timelines for investigations and the creation of a ten-person Handschu Committee, whose task was to oversee the New York Police Department's compliance with the consent decree.[43] As part of the settlement, the New York Police Department, while not admitting any wrongdoing, agreed to prohibit investigations where race, religion, or ethnicity functions as a "substantial or motivating factor" and to launch any subsequent investigations based only on "actionable intelligence" of potential terrorist activity. The New York Police Department also agreed to appoint a civilian to monitor its counter-terrorism efforts and to pay $1.6 million to cover the plaintiffs' legal fees.[44] The revised consent decree is notable for its mandate that this civilian representative must never have been an employee of the New York Police Department, whose tasks include reporting all objections to the New York Police Department; informing the Handschu court of all systematic and repeated violations of the revised guidelines; and although being unable unilaterally to block investigations, serving as an important whistleblower in relation to police misconduct.[45] The settlement also entailed very strong language that the New York Police Department "[did] not, have not, and will not rely on" Silber and Bhatt's *Radicalization in the West*, briefly described earlier, and that the New York Police Department would purge the said document from its website.[46]

This section aims to analyze the jurisprudence that results from *Raza v. New York*, and to assess whether, and to what extent, its results constituted a legal and cultural counter-narrative to the narrative espoused by the culture of jihadi cool, and its corollary, that the practice of Islam is the gateway to self-radicalization. The result, as I demonstrate, is far from unambiguous, largely because both sides relied upon essentially the same assumption, which, as shown above, is still one of jihadi cool/chic's assumptions: that Islam functions as the gateway to radicalization.

The Battleground of Expedited Discovery: The Importance of a Discriminatory Animus in Equal Protection

Given the amount of popular press that *Raza v. New York* received, one may be surprised to see that the case did not move beyond the issue of expedited discovery. Nevertheless, the pre-trial pace and the flurry at which the case moved reveal how much was at stake for all parties. The plaintiffs filed for expedited discovery while the defendants, within a day of filing their answer, filed for bifurcated discovery; briefly outlined, the defendants questioned the plaintiffs' standing and whether they had actually suffered constitutional violations.[47] The plaintiffs made it clear, through their requests for expedited discovery, that they sought a wide range of documents and information focused on the New York Police Department's "investigative policies and activities relating to all Muslim individuals and organizations, and relating to all non-Muslim individuals and organizations, where the policy or activity is or was based on the individual's or organization's religious speech, beliefs, practices and activities."[48] In turn, the defendants' response used the standard objections based on a lack of relevance, overbreadth, and undue burden; stressed the "heightened law enforcement sensitivity" of the information; and argued that the plaintiffs had failed to meet the standard required for expedited discovery.[49]

There were four causes of action raised by the plaintiffs, who were three Muslim individuals, two mosques, and a nonprofit Muslim organization; these were violations of: (1) the Equal Protection Clause of the Fourteenth Amendment, (2) the Free Exercise Clause of the First Amendment, (3) the Establishment Clause of the First Amendment, and (4) the right to exercise their religion freely under Articles One and Three of the New York State Constitution.[50]

It is important to note that this case was never decided on the merits. The standard of review in relation to whether the plaintiffs had met the standard justifying expedited review was an abuse of discretion—an extremely permissive standard.[51] The court found that the plaintiffs did not meet the required standard because the plaintiffs' "claims of fear and stigmatization, which are largely unsupported," did not "demonstrate good cause warranting expedited discovery."[52] Because it became clear that the parties could not even agree on a discovery schedule, the court ultimately decided simply to impose a timeline for discovery that attempted to strike a balance between the competing pleadings of the parties.[53]

As to the plaintiffs' discovery requests, the court attempted a complex balancing act by granting the plaintiffs' request for documents that were directly about them; if, however, other non-plaintiffs were included, the defendants were allowed to redact these names provided the defendants indicated: (1) whether these were Muslim and (2) whether these had been the subject of surveillance or an investigation.[54] To make the balancing act even more nuanced, the court required another limit point: the data had to be disclosed "unless the disclosure of this information would indirectly reveal the subject's identity or threaten to undermine an ongoing investigation."[55]

The court also granted the plaintiffs' request for general charts and information related to the structure, organization, general operations, and purpose or mission of the New York Police Department's Intelligence Division; the limit point was "specific activities" of this division.[56] But the court did its most careful analysis in relation to what it considered the heart of the matter: the plaintiffs' request for "Intelligence Division reports, assessments, presentations, memoranda, policy statements, operational directives, strategy documents, and training material" that reflected a basis for, or were relevant to, the decision to engage in surveillance or investigations on: (1) Islam, its adherents or schools of thought, including but not limited to Salafism, (2) Non-Islamic religions, their adherents, or their schools of thought, and (3) "Ancestries of interest," which were already made available in an Intelligence Division presentation.[57]

As to relevance, the burden lay with the plaintiffs to prove their Equal Protection and First Amendment claims, that the defendants conducted investigations or surveillance with a discriminatory purpose or intent. *Ashcroft v. Iqbal*, 556 US 662, 677, 129 S. Ct. 1937, 173 L. Ed. 2D 868 (2009); *Vill. Of Arlington Heights v. Metro. Hous. Dev. Corp.*, 429 US 252, 270, 97 S. Ct. 555, 50 L. Ed. 2D 450 (1977) (both cases requiring, in relation to proving invidious discrimination in violation of the First and Fifth Amendments, that the plaintiff prove that the defendant acted with or was motivated by a discriminatory purpose).[58]

As an outward manifestation of this discriminatory purpose, the plaintiffs could either show that a law or policy "expressly classifie[d] persons on the basis of race"[59] or show that a facially neutral law or policy was applied in an intentionally discriminatory way. Alternatively, the plaintiffs could also demonstrate that a facially neutral statute or policy had an adverse effect and was motivated by a "discriminatory animus."[60] *Brown v. City of Oneonta*, 221 F.3d 329, 337 (2d Cir. 1999) (quoting *Hayden v. Cnty. Of Nassau*, 180 F.3d 42, 48 (2d 1999) (internal citations omitted)).[61]

The plaintiffs, through their pleadings, indicated that they intended to use one or two ways indicated in *Brown*:[62] (1) through an express classification theory—that is, by showing that the New York Police Department overtly classified Muslims by "adopting a policy of singling them out for heightened policy scrutiny," or (2) via a discriminatory application theory—that is, "by showing that [the plaintiffs] were subject to [New York Police Department] investigations of unequal and unwarranted scope, duration and invasiveness as a result of their religious beliefs and activities."[63]

The defendants, through their answers, "effectively conceded the relevance of the [New York Police Department]'s strategy and policy documents," but argued that the plaintiffs were not entitled to access to these documents during the discovery phase.[64] This was because, the defendants argued, the plaintiffs "[had to] first establish an underlying constitutional violation, in other words, they [had to] establish that the [New York Police Department] had an improper motive" in investigating them.[65] However, the *Raza* court disagreed, holding that there was a clear distinction between the Fourth Amendment and an Equal Protection claim; it stated:

> In contrast to a claim under the Fourth Amendment, the existence of criminal predication, e.g., reasonable suspicion or probable cause, does not automatically defeat an Equal Protection claim. An Equal Protection claim can be established where there exist "mixed motives" for the challenged government conduct.[66] *See Hunter v. Underwood*, 471 US 222, 225, 105 S. Ct. 1916, 85 L. Ed. 2D 222 (1985); *Vill. of Arlington Heights.*, 429 US At 270; *Mt. Healthy City School Dist. Bd. Of Educ. v. Doyle*, 429 US 274, 287, 97 S. Ct. 568, 50 L. Ed. 2D 471 (1977). Even if Defendants' investigations of Plaintiffs were supported by criminal predication, if those investigations were improperly influenced by Plaintiffs' religion, they may be unconstitutional.[67]

As a basis for this holding, the court cited *Whren v. United States*, 517 US 806, 813, 116 S. Ct. 1769, 135 L.E. 89 (1996), which distinguished between actions based on the Fourth Amendment, where the defendants' "[s]ubjective intentions play no role," and actions based on the Equal Protection Clause, which are based on an "intentionally discriminatory application" of the law.[68] The court also relied upon two other cases: (1) *United States v. Avery*, 137 F.3d 343, 352 (6th Cir. 1997), which held that the "Equal Protection Clause of the Fourteenth Amendment provides citizens a degree of protection independent of the Fourth Amendment protection against unreasonable searches and seizures"[69] and (2) *United States v. Scopo*, 19 F.3d 777, 786 (2d Cir. 1994) (Newman, C.J., concurring), which stated: "Though the Fourth Amendment permits a pretext arrest, if otherwise supported by probable cause, the Equal Protection Clause still imposes restraint on impermissibly class-based discriminations."[70]

The court went on to stress that in cases involving a "mixed motive" or "dual motivation[s]," where at least one factor is improper or discriminatory, the existence of other motives, even if proper, does not preclude a cause of action based on Equal Protection.[71] See, for example, *Mt. Healthy City Sch. Dist. Bd. Of Educ. v. Doyle*, 429 US 274, 287, 97 S. Ct. 568, 50 L. Ed., 2d 471 (1977); *United States v. City of Yonkers*, 96 F.3d 600, 611–12 (2d Cir. 1996);

Howard v. Senkowski, 986 F.2d 24, 29–30 (2d Cir, 1993); *Vill. Of Arlington Heights v. Metro. Hous, Dev. Corp.*, 429 US 252, 270, 97 S. Ct. 555, 50 L. Ed. 2D 450 (1977).[72] Nevertheless, plaintiffs were required to prove, via a preponderance of evidence, that the alleged "discrimination was a substantial or motivating factor" for the government's or in this case, the New York Police Department's actions.[73] See, for example, *Hunter v. Underwood*, 471 US 222, 225, 105 S. Ct. 1916, 85 L. Ed. 2D 222 (1985).[74]

The court acknowledged that it was striking into relatively unexplored territory by stating:

> The Court recognizes that, other than in the selective prosecution model, the application of the "dual motivation" framework to allegedly discriminatory *law enforcement* activities is not well established. However, the Second Circuit's decision in *Pyke v. Cuomo* supports the proposition that a plaintiff can bring an Equal Protection claim with respect to law enforcement conduct *without* alleging selective prosecution.[75]

In selective prosecution cases, a plaintiff must both allege and prove that similarly situated persons outside of his or her protected class were treated differently; this is called the "Armstrong Rule."[76] However, as the *Pyke* court explained, when no claim of selective prosecution is made, the Armstrong Rule does not apply.[77] *Pyke v. Cuomo* therefore stands for the rule that "a plaintiff can bring an Equal Protection claim with respect to law enforcement conduct without alleging selective prosecution."[78]

In *Pyke v. Cuomo*, residents of the Mohawk Indian reservation in upstate New York claimed that the State was discriminatorily withholding police protection on the reservation.[79] The district court granted summary judgment to the defendants because the plaintiffs had failed to show disparate treatment and had not raised the issue of express racial classification; nevertheless, the Second Circuit vacated and remanded.[80]

The Second Circuit panel specifically stated:

> A plaintiff alleging an equal protection claim under a theory of discriminatory application of the law, or under a theory of discriminatory motivation underlying a facially neutral policy or statute, generally need not plead or show the disparate treatment of other similarly situated individuals.[81]

Thus, the panel distinguished between Equal Protection causes of action claiming selective prosecution, which require a showing that disparate treatment of similarly situated individuals occurred, and causes of action that "challeng[e] a law or policy that contains an express, racial classification" for which "it is not necessary to allege the existence of a similarly situated non-minority group."[82] In part, the panel's decision was grounded in the fact that it is often objectively difficult to make direct comparisons between different groups (even if similarly situated) in order to demonstrate animus.[83] Finally, the panel also expounded on the Circuit's holding in *Brown*, stating that the rule that Equal Protection claims do not require a showing of disparate treatment is not limited purely to challenges to policies with express racial classifications. The *Pyke* panel stated:

> We now clarify—a plaintiff who, as in *Brown*, alleges an express racial classification, or alleges that a facially neutral law or policy has been applied in an intentionally discriminatory race-based manner, or that a facially neutral statute or policy with an adverse effect was motivated by discriminatory animus, is not obligated to show a better treated, similarly situated group of individuals of a different race in order to establish a claim of denial of equal protection.[84]

Thus, building on the *Pyke* jurisprudence, the *Raza* court concluded that the plaintiffs could proceed with their Equal Protection claim based on the New York Police Department's allegedly discriminatory investigation and surveillance of the plaintiffs without needing to allege selective prosecution and without having to prove disparate treatment of a similarly situated non-Muslim group.[85]

Hence, since evidence of the New York Police Department's intent in relation to their surveillance or investigations of the plaintiffs was crucial to the plaintiffs' Equal Protection allegations, the *Raza* court concluded that the plaintiffs' discovery requests regarding any New York Police Department policy or program involving the investigation of Muslims as a group based, whether in whole or in part, on their religion, were necessary.[86] Without access to such discovery, the *Raza* court reasoned, the plaintiffs would be unjustly "pre[-]emptively and irreparably prohibited from proving the [d]efendants' alleged discriminatory intent was a motivating factor in the investigation and surveillance of [the] [p]laintiffs."[87] To the defense's objection that this would allow an unlimited "fishing expedition," the court pointed out that attachments to the plaintiffs' submissions strongly suggested that the New York Police Department did have documents relevant to this inquiry, as evidenced in references to either the Taqwa mosque or Plaintiff Elshinawy, or both.[88]

The *Raza* court also emphasized certain flaws in the New York Police Department's reasoning. First, the defense presumed what the supposed outcome of the discovery would be: that any documents beyond those that specifically reference the plaintiffs "could never be relevant to a showing of discriminatory intent with respect to [d]efendants' investigations of [p] laintiffs. In other words, the defense assumed that the revelation of criminal predication (reasonable suspicion or probable cause) for their investigations would automatically preclude or supercede a finding of discriminatory intent."[89] As the court stated, this would so curtail the evidence to which plaintiffs would have access and make it even more difficult for them to meet the standard required to prove a violation of Equal Protection.

Second, the defense also tended to construe the purposes of discovery too narrowly, which was contrary to the existing jurisprudence regarding the proper scope of discovery, which encouraged principles of broad discovery, especially where proving discriminatory intent was required. *See, for example, Hunter v. Underwood,* 471 US 222, 228, 105 S. Ct. 1916, 85 L. Ed. 2D 222 (1985) ("Proving the motivation behind official action is often a problematic undertaking."); *Vill. Of Arlington Heights v. Metro. Hous. Dev. Corp.*, 429 US 252, 266, 97 S. Ct. 555, 50 L. Ed. 2D 450 (1977) ("Determining whether invidious discriminatory purpose was a motivating factor demands a sensitive inquiry into such circumstantial and direct evidence of intent as may be available."); *Gray v. Bd. of Higher Educ., City of New York*, 692 F.2d 901, 906 (2d Cir. 1982) (reversing district court's denial of discovery in part because "[t]he district court minimized the importance of appellant's discovery needs" in relation to evidence of intent and finding that "if unable to engage in discovery, [the plaintiff] cannot prove intent, and without proof of intent, he has no case"). The need for not only such broad but also "sensitive" parameters of discovery was made even more so in relation to Equal Protection claims because there is seldom a "smoking gun" that shows direct proof of such animus; usually, plaintiffs have to prove discriminatory intent via the "cumulative weight of circumstantial evidence."[90]

Third, precluding plaintiffs from obtaining any information regarding an overarching "Muslim surveillance program" would severely and unfairly hamper them from meeting the standard required: that discrimination based on their religion was at least in part a motivating factor in the New York Police Department's decisions to conduct surveillance or investigations on them.[91] *See, for example, Brown v. City of Oneonta*, 221 F.3d 329, 337 (2d Cir. 1999) (affirming the denial of Equal Protection claims because the plaintiffs failed to show "any law or policy that contain[ed] an 'express racial classification'").

The New York Police Department, in its arguments regarding the need for bifurcated discovery, relied heavily on *Dinler v. City of New York*, 607 F.3d 923 (2d Cir. 2010). In *Dinler*, the court issued a writ of mandamus that reversed the district court's order compelling the New York Police Department to produce intelligence reports written by undercover officers covering potential security threats in relation to the Republican National Convention. However, the *Raza* court distinguished *Raza* from *Dinler* because in *Dinler*, the issues involved violations of the Fourth Amendment (which rendered defendants' motives irrelevant), the challenge of only the defendants' arrests and detentions, and the upholding of law enforcement privilege.[92]

In contrast, as explained above, in *Raza*, the issues revolved around Equal Protection, which necessarily entailed proving of a discriminatory animus as the motive for the New York Police Department's surveillance or investigations and the challenge of not only the plaintiffs' surveillance and investigations but also of a larger "Muslim surveillance program."[93] Furthermore, the *Raza* court reasoned, in *Dinler*, mandamus was the only relief possible because the district court had ordered the production of documents that were subject to law enforcement privilege.[94] In contrast, in *Raza*, the court stated that the order did not "impinge upon [the New York Police Department]'s ability to claim law enforcement privilege with respect to particular documents, which [could still] be addressed on a document-specific basis."[95]

The *Raza* court also carefully weighed whether the New York Police Department's request for bifurcated discovery could be granted and arrived at a similar conclusion: even if, *arguendo*, a bifurcated approach would reveal the existence of reasonable suspicion or probable cause for surveillance or investigation, the court would still be compelled to require further discovery regarding whether such a broad-based policy that discriminated against Muslims as a group existed.[96] And even if, arguendo, no evidence of a "Muslim surveillance program" could be found in this initial phase, precisely because of the broad construction of principles of discovery in relation to the existence of a discriminatory intent that an Equal Protection claim requires, the court would still be equally compelled to move into the second phase.[97] This was rendered even clearer because the New York Police Department failed to produce any relevant case law involving Equal Protection "in which a court dismissed the plaintiff's complaint based solely on a finding of probable cause."[98] The *Raza* court further explained that the existence of reasonable suspicion or probable cause, as a matter of law, did not itself resolve the "possibility of causation between the allegedly discriminatory policy" and the plaintiffs' surveillance or investigations.[99] Furthermore, this type of determination of whether legitimate criminal predication existed, according to the *Raza* court, should be made at the end, and not at the start, of the discovery process.[100] The *Raza* court thus concluded, emphasizing the primacy of a discriminatory animus:

> Discriminatory intent is at the core of Plaintiffs' claims—and the existence of a formal policy or practice, if one exists, certainly would be relevant to Plaintiffs' claims. Plaintiffs are entitled to seek evidence that would tend to show Defendants' discriminatory intent in investigating them. Federal Rule of Civil Procedure 26(b)(1) provides for broad discovery into evidence "regarding any nonprivileged matter that is relevant to a party's claim or defense" and that "the court may order discovery of *any matter relevant* to the subject matter involved in the action." Here, if Defendants have a policy, whether formally adopted or adhered to in pattern or practice, its existence would make it more likely that Plaintiffs themselves were investigated on the basis of their religion, potentially in violation of constitutional rights. Accordingly, artificially limiting discovery in the manner suggested by Defendants, to wit, *exclusively* to documents referring to Plaintiffs, would be inadequate under these circumstances.[101]

Nevertheless, keeping in mind the potential burden and expense to be incurred by the New York Police Department in complying with the plaintiffs' Request Number 4, the *Raza* court tailored the request to include only:

> *Intelligence Division documents containing operational directives, presentations, memoranda, strategy initiatives, training procedures, and policies*, concerning any of the following as a basis for, or a factor considered in, deciding to engage in Surveillance or Investigations:
>
> a. Islam, its adherents, or its schools of thought, including but not limited to Salafis or Salafism;
> b. Non-Islamic religions, their adherents, or their schools of thought with *any alleged link or connection to terrorism*;
> c. "Ancestries of interest" as identified as an Intelligence Division presentation available at: http://bit.ly/1alT2ss2A.[102]

In contrast, the plaintiffs' requests (numbers five and six) for various documents from 2004 until 2013 regarding the investigation or surveillance of any and all Muslims, and all non-Muslims, on the basis of their religious beliefs or practices were denied.[103] In brief, the *Raza* court agreed with the New York Police Department's conclusion (but not rationale) that there was no meaningful way to compare all Muslims who were investigated (including but not only the plaintiffs) to all non-Muslims because "[g]iven the myriad of factors that go into every investigation and, indeed, every step of every investigation, attempting to compare hundreds, if not thousands, of different investigations to each other to discern a pattern of disparate treatment of similarly situated individuals would be futile."[104]

Even more importantly, as explained earlier, the demonstration of an express racial classification or of a facially neutral law or policy that has been applied in an intentionally race- or religion-based discriminatory manner obviated the need for a showing of a better-treated similarly situated group of persons of a different race or religion to prove an Equal Protection violation.[105] Thus, these requests were of very limited probative value and would be "impossibly burdensome" to the New York Police Department in terms of resources, manpower, time, and expenses.[106]

The plaintiffs' request numbers seven, eight, and nine were similar to items five and six outlined above and were treated similarly. These were requests for statistics concerning Muslim individuals or organizations versus non-Muslim individuals or organizations who were criminally charged as a result of the activities of the Intelligence Division. The New York Police Department argued that they did not classify their investigations according to religion and thus were unable to produce these statistics.[107] The *Raza* court agreed, citing in part to *Scherbakovskiy v. Da Capo Al Fine, Ltd.*, 490 F.3d 130, 138 (2d Cir. 2007) ("a party is not obliged to produce, at the risk of sanctions, documents that it does not possess or cannot obtain").[108] Furthermore, as explained earlier, even if such statistics existed, because of the complex nature of the way decisions are made in relation to investigations, such data were of limited probative value and relevance, and were not even necessary for the plaintiffs to prove an Equal Protection violation.[109]

The plaintiffs also requested that the New York Police Department respond to an interrogatory regarding whether they had a database or means of electronic analysis that would enable the plaintiffs to sort through data from 2004 to 2013 regarding Muslim individuals or organizations as opposed to non-Muslim individuals or organizations who were either kept under surveillance, investigated, or criminally charged based on religious affiliation, speech, belief, or activities.[110] Because the New York Police Department simply flatly denied that such a database existed, and provided no legal justification, the court granted the plaintiffs' request that the interrogatory be answered.[111]

Nevertheless, the *Raza* court closed with an acknowledgment of the importance of protecting the privileged information related to ongoing or contemplated investigations; the privacy of individuals who were investigated but not charged; and the safety and efficacy of undercover police officers and confidential informants.[112] Eventually, even if the plaintiffs' request for expedited discovery was partially granted and the New York Police Department's request for bifurcated discovery was denied, given the degree of fractiousness in litigation between both parties, the *Raza* court took it upon itself to set the Discovery and Briefing Schedule as outlined below:

- 2 weeks from order—Parties serve their document requests and interrogatories.
- 1 month thereafter—Defendants respond to Document Requests #1—#3 and the Interrogatory; and Plaintiffs respond to Defendants' discovery requests, if any.
- 1 month thereafter—Defendants respond to Plaintiffs' Document Request #4.
- 3 weeks thereafter—Parties serve deposition notices.
- 2 months thereafter—Depositions completed.
- 2 weeks thereafter—Parties serve requests for admission.
- 3 weeks thereafter—Parties respond to requests for admission.
- 4 weeks thereafter—Parties serve their motion for a preliminary injunction on Defendants.
- 4 weeks thereafter—Defendants serve their response to the preliminary injunction motion on Plaintiffs.
- 3 weeks thereafter—Plaintiffs serve their reply regarding the preliminary injunction motion on Defendants. Parties file their preliminary injunction submissions with the Court.[113]

The jurisprudence that therefore results from *Raza v. New York* is noteworthy principally for pointing out a key difference between Equal Protection claims and Fourth Amendment claims. Equal Protection claims allow for a broader application of discovery principles because of the plaintiffs' hurdle of proving discriminatory intent, unlike searches and seizures where discriminatory intent is not generally considered relevant, based on existing case law. Interestingly, at least at the level of discovery, a civil, rather than criminal, case afforded greater protection for a class-action suit for nongovernmental entities that had banded together.

However, it is wise to note the disparities between the popular representations of *Raza v. New York* and the actual case law that resulted from it. *Raza v. New York* has been popularly hailed either as a defeat of the pseudo-scientism of the Radicalization Model as applied to the criminalization of the practice of Islam as the gateway to self-radicalization, or as a capitulation to the onslaught of forces of political correctness. Both popular narratives, in certain senses, aspire to be master narratives that ironically result from precisely accepting the premise that flows from jihadi cool/chic's siren song: that there is no way out of the devil's bargain in relation to the practice of Islam, as its adherents are framed to be marginalized culturally, socially, and legally by "Western" institutional structures. This is, in some ways, hardly surprising, as modes of popularization tend to hyperbolize or oversimplify, concentrate, and reduce into a sound bite what is complex and nuanced. Modes of popularization in the virtual world also lead to a splintering of worlds, where virtual communities can create insular universes that screen out dissent, leading to something resembling a collective neurosis.

The legal narrative that results from *Raza v. New York*, in contrast, seems of significance mainly to legal tacticians or constitutional scholars because of its emphasis on delineating the differences between the Fourth Amendment (involving searches and seizures) and the Fourteenth Amendment (involving Equal Protection). There is thus a need to form a bridge between these two spheres: the sphere of the courtroom, where the exoteric and specialized generate the jurisprudence and practice of law, and the sphere of the public marketplace of culture, where the exoteric becomes simplified and reduced into tweets or posts in echo chambers of elective microcommunities.

Ludwik Fleck's *The Genesis and Development of a Scientific Fact*[114] provides a parallel model because arguably, the history and philosophy of science provide fruitful models for studying both the progressive and regressive aspects of modes of popularization. Briefly summarized, Fleck posited that the conversion of a scientific observation, initially within the arena of the exoteric inhabited by specialists, to a "fact," which resides in the esoteric sphere occupied by the "normal" sphere of the everyday, occurs through a translation or form of metaphoric reinvention by a scientific popularizer—one capable of proverbially dancing across the realms of both the exoteric and the esoteric. An example of this would be Stephen Jay Gould,[115] whose popular writings on saltationism or punctuated equilibrium (i.e., that evolution proceeds via sudden, unpredictable leaps rather than gradual and cumulative increments) did much to educate the public on evolutionism.[116] Thus, analogously, what may be necessary is a fresh new way to think through how individuals and nongovernmental actors critically interact with, rather than passively consume, the onslaught of revolving and competing master narratives. For Chapter 4,

I briefly sketch an outline for such an approach through a "poethics" of witnessing.

To summarize briefly, Chapter 2 has sought to contribute to jurisprudence debates insofar as it presented in great technical detail the relevant case law that enabled the *Raza* court to distinguish between Fourth Amendment and Equal Protection litigation in granting discovery to plaintiffs seeking to establish discrimination claims. Of particular import was the discussion of the historical background that preceded this litigation, particularly in connection with the collaboration between intelligence agencies and the NYPD, as well as the critical review of the theories of radicalization and their assumptions, since these undergird the government policies and procedures that seek to counter this process. This analysis of underlying assumptions is of immense importance to a poethics of witnessing, which the final chapter lays out.

Notes

1 Phil Gurski, *The Threat from Within: Recognizing Al Qaeda-Inspired Radicalization and Terrorism in the West* (Lanham, MD: Rowman & Littlefield Publishers, 2016), 8.

2 Gurski points out that "The West," as constructed in jihadi cool/chic's narrative, refers to "not only the 'traditional' West (the United States, UK, Canada, and Western Europe) but also Israel, Russia, China, India, and anyone else seen as an enemy of Islam. Muslim countries closely allied to the West—Saudi Arabia, Jordan, and so on—are usually folded into this group." Ibid. at 9.

3 Shadi Hamid and Rashid Dar, "Islamism, Salafism, and Jihadism: A Primer," *The Brookings Institution*, at 3, https://www.brookings.edu/blog/markaz/2016/07/15/islamism-salafism-and-jihadism-a-primer/.

4 Ibid.

5 Ibid.

6 Ibid. at 4.

7 Ibid.

8 Ajit Maan, *Counter Terrorism: Narrative Strategies* (Lanham, MD: University Press of America, 2015), 19–30.

9 Amna Akbar, "National Security's Broken Windows," *UCLA Law Review* 62 (2015): 834, 837–907.

10 Mitchell D. Silber and Arvin Bhatt, "Radicalization in the West: The Homegrown Threat," *New York City Police Department* (2007), at 57–82, accessed April 2, 2015, http://www.nyc.gov/html/nypd/downloads/pdf/public_information/NYPD_Report-Radicalization_in_the_West.pdf.

11 Ibid. at 23–56.

12 Ibid. at 57–82.

13 Karen D. Keys-Turner, "The Violent Islamic Radicalization Process: A Framework for Understanding" (December 2011), M.A. thesis, Naval Postgraduate School, Monterey, CA (on file with Defense Technical Information Center, ADA556429), at 44.

14 This summary of Silber and Bhatt's model of radicalization is adapted from: Picart, *American Self-Radicalizing Terrorists*, at 15–16.

15 Silber and Bhatt, *Radicalization in the West*, at 6.

16 Ibid.

17 Ibid.

18 Senators Joseph Lieberman and Susan Collins, "Violent Islamist Extremism, The Internet, and the Homegrown Terrorist Threat, Majority and Minority Staff Report," *US Senate Committee on Homeland Security and Governmental Affairs,* May 8, 2008), accessed September 10, 2016, http://hsgac.senate.gov/public/_files/IslamistReport.pdf.

19 Silber and Bhatt, "Radicalization in the West," at 7.

20 Andrew Silke, "Holy Warriors: Exploring the Psychological Processes of Jihadi Radicalization," *European Journal of Criminology* 5 (2008): 99, 110.

21 "Radicalization, Information Sharing and Community Outreach: Protecting the Homeland from Homegrown Terror," Hearing Before the Senate Committee on Intelligence, Information Sharing, and Terrorism Risk Assessment of the House Committee on Homeland Security, 110th Cong. 2 (2007) (testimony of John Neu, Chief of Police Department), http://hsc-democrats.house.gov/SiteDocuments/20070405120653-23987.pdf; "The Role of Local Enforcement in Countering Violent Islamic Extremism," Hearing Before the Senate Committee on Homeland Security and Governmental Affairs, 110th Cong. 1 (2007) (statement for the record by Maj. Thomas Dailey, Kansas City, Mo. Police Department, Homeland Security Division), http://hsgac.senate.gov/public/index.cfm?FuseAction=Files.View&FileStore_id=81c0387a-e20c-4b02

-8257-6885b0e1c3f5; Intelligence Bureau, N.J. Office of Homeland Sec. & Preparedness, "Homegrown Plots: New York 2009 and Fort Dix," 2009, at 1, http://info.publicintelligence.net/Homegrown%20Plots-New%20York%202009%20and%20Fort%Dix.pdf.

22 Press Release, "Senate Homeland Security Committee Hearing Examines Islamic Radicalism Inside United States," *Senate Committee on Homeland Security and Governmental Affairs*, March 14, 2007, https://web.archive.org/web/20110311211755/http:/hsgac.senate.gov/public/index.cfm?FuseAction=Press.MajorityNews&ContentRecord_id=d0543abb-0376-4a5c-9a4e-09649e2ed8ef.

23 Press Release, Peter King, "What's Radicalizing Muslim Americans?," *Homeland Security Committee*, December 19, 2010, http://homeland.house.gov/press-release/newsday-king-whats-radicalizing-muslim-americans.

24 *See, e.g.*, Anne Barnard and Alan Feuer, "Outraged, and Outrageous," *The New York Times*, October 8, 2010, at MB1, http://www.nytimes.com/2010/10/10/nyregion/10geller.html; and Steven Emerson, "The New York Times: Making the World Safe for Terrorism," *The Counter Jihad Report*, May 14, 2014, https://web.archive.org/web/20140519160238/http://counterjihadreport.com:80/category/nypd/.

25 Veena Dubal, "The Demise of Community Policing? The Impact of Post-9/11 Federal Surveillance Programs on Local Law Enforcement," *Asian American Law Journal* 19, no. 1 (2012): 35, https://lawcat.berkeley.edu/record/1124968?ln=en&v=pdf; Faiza Patel, "Rethinking Radicalization," *Brennan Center for Justice at the N.Y.U. School of Law*, March 8, 2011, at 3, https://www.brennancenter.org/publication/rethinking-radicalization; Aziz Z. Huq, "Modeling Terrorist Radicalization," *Duke Forum for Law and Social Change* 2 (2010): 39, 39–69, http://dflsc.law.duke.edu/article/modeling-terrorist-radicalization/.

26 Adam Goldman and Matt Apuzzo, "NYPD Secretly Designated Entire Mosques as Terrorism Organizations," *Huffington Post*, August 28, 2013, http://www.huffingtonpost.com/2013/08/28/nypd-spying-mosques_n_3827567.html.

27 Complaint, *Raza v. City of New York*, No. 13-cv-3448-PKC-JMA, 5–9 (E.D.N.Y. June 18, 2013), https://www.aclu.org/national-security/raza-v-city-new-york-complaint.

28 *See Handschu v. Police Department of N.Y.*, 219 F. Supp. 388 (S.D.N.Y. 2016).

29 Goldman and Apuzzo, "NYPD Secretly Designated Entire Mosques."

30 Chris Hawley, "Law May Not be on Muslims' Side in NYPD Intel Case," *Associated Press, San Diego Union Tribune*, November 7, 2011, 11:31 PM, https://www.sandiegouniontribune.com/sdut-law-may-not-be-on-muslims-side-in-nypd-intel-case-2011nov07-story.html.

31 Matt Apuzzo and Adam Goldman, *Enemies Within: Inside the NYPD's Secret Spying Unit and Bin Laden's Final Plot Against America* (New York: Simon & Schuster, 2013); David Crary, "AP Series About NYPD Surveillance Wins Pulitzer," *Associated Press*, April 16, 2012, https://www.ap.org/ap-in-the-news/2012/ap-series-about-nypd-surveillance-wins-pulitzer.

32 Adam Goldman and Matt Apuzzo, "CIA to Pull Officer from NYPD After Internal Probe," Associated Press, *Times West Virginian*, January 6, 2012, accessed July 27, 2014, https://www.timeswv.com/news/national_news/cia-to-pull-officer-from-nypd-after-internal-probe/article_ce398add-de8a-5452-acff-6fc740554c7f.html.

33 Ibid.

34 Matt Apuzzo and Adam Goldman, "With CIA Help, NYPD Moves Covertly in Muslim Areas," Associated Press, August 24, 2011, https://www.pulitzer.org/winners/matt-apuzzo-adam-goldman-eileen-sullivan-and-chris-hawley.

35 Ibid. "The department has gotten some its officers deputized as federal marshals, allowing them to work out of state. But often, there's no specific jurisdiction at all."

36 Ibid.

37 Ibid.

38 Goldman and Apuzzo, *CIA to Pull Officer from NYPD*.

39 Michael Calderone, "AP's Matt Apuzzo and Adam Goldman Crack Open Secretive Institutions, from NYPD to CIA," *Huffington Post*, September 3, 2013, 05:39 PM, https://www.huffpost.com/entry/ap-nypd-matt-apuzzo-adam-goldman_n_3861444.

40 *Raza v. City of New York*, 998 F. Supp. 2D 70 (E.D.N.Y. 2013).

41 There is a long history to this lawsuit. Briefly summarized, in 1971, Barbara Handschu joined other plaintiffs in a class-action lawsuit against the New York Police Department, challenging the police department's surveillance strategies or tactics, and in specific, the use of files or dossiers on activists and its undercover infiltration of political organizations. In 1985, a settlement and consent decree generated the Handschu Committee, which was a panel designated to oversee covert New York Police Department surveillance operations. *See Handschu*

v. Special Services Div., 605 F. Supp. 1384 (S.D.N.Y. 1985). The Handschu agreement theoretically requires that undercover personnel must have "fact-specific" reasons for their necessity and proscribes the targeting of suspects for their political preferences. Ibid. at 1391–2. Nevertheless, these protections were eroded gradually. For example, in 2003, the Handschu court removed all restrictions on New York Police Department investigative activity. *See Handschu v. Special Servs. Div.*, 273 F. Supp. 273 F. Supp. 2d. 345 (S.D.N.Y. 2003). Additionally, in 2007, the Handschu court amended the consent decree by requiring that plaintiffs demonstrate a pattern of systematic violation for the court to be able to enjoin any New York Police Department policy. *See Handschu v. Special Servs. Div.*, 2007 US Dist. LEXIS 43176 at 67 (S.D.N.Y. 2007). The overall effect was to essentially allow the New York Police Department to ignore the modified Handschu agreement, ironically expanding its surveillance powers and rendering ineffective the Handschu Committee's authority. *See* Ibid.

42 *Handschu v. Police Dep't of N.Y.*, 905 F. Supp. 2d 555 (S.D.N.Y. 2012).

43 *Handschu v. Police Dep't*, 241 F. Supp. 3d 433, 438 (S.D.N.Y. 2017).

44 Sarah E. Jones, "Spy vs. Constitution: New York City Police Agree to Settlement in Muslim Surveillance Case," *Americans United*, January 8, 2016.

45 *Handschu v. Police Dep't*, 241 F. Supp. 433, 438, 440 (S.D.N.Y. 2017).

46 Adam Kredo, "Court Requires NYPD to Purge Documents on Terrorists Inside U.S.," *The Washington Free Beacon*, January 18, 2016, https://freebeacon.com/national-security/court-requires-nypd-purge-docs-terrorists-inside-us/.

47 *Raza v. City of New York*, 998 F. Supp. at 73–4.

48 Ibid. at 74.

49 Ibid. at 74–5.

50 Ibid. at 73.

51 *In re Subpoena Issued to Dennis Friedman*, 350 F.3d 65, 69 (2d Cir. 2003); *Metro. Life Ins. Co. v. RJR Nabisco, Inc.*, 906 F.2d 884, 891 (2d Cir. 1990); *United Parcel Serv. Of Am., Inc. v. The Net. Inc.*, 222 F.R.D. 69,71 (E.D.N.Y. 2004).

52 *Raza v. City of New York*, 998 F. Supp. at 75.

53 Ibid. at 76, note 2.

54 Ibid. at 76–7.

55 Ibid. at 77.

56 Ibid. at 77–8.

57 Ibid. at 78.

58 Ibid.

59 Ibid.

60 Ibid.

61 Ibid.

62 *Brown v. City of Oneonta*, 221 F. 3d 329, 337 (2d Cir. 1999).

63 *Raza v. City of New York*, 998 F. Supp. at 78.

64 Ibid.

65 Ibid.

66 Ibid.

67 Ibid. at 79.

68 Ibid.

69 Ibid.

70 Ibid.

71 Ibid.

72 Ibid. at 80.

73 Ibid.

74 Ibid.

75 Ibid., emphasis in original.

76 *United States v. Armstrong*, 517 US 456, 465, 116 S. Ct. 1480, 134 L. Ed. 2D 687 (1996).

77 *Pyke v. Cuomo*, 258 F.3d 107, 109 (2d Cir. 2001).

78 *Raza v. City of New York*, 998 F. Supp. at 80.

79 *Pyke v. Cuomo*, 258 F.3d 107, 108 (2d Cir. 2001).

80 Ibid. at 108, 110.

81 Ibid. at 108–9.

82 Ibid. at 109 (quoting *Brown v. City of Oneonta*, 221 F.3d 329, 337 (2d Cir. 1999)).

83 Ibid. (quoting Ibid.)

84 Ibid. at 110 (2d Cir. 2001).

85 *Raza v. City of New York*, 998 F. Supp. at 81.

86 Ibid. at 81.

87 Ibid.

88 Ibid.

89 Ibid. at 82.

90 *Rosen v. Thornburgh*, 928 F.2d 528, 533 (2d Cir. 1991); *see also Chambers v. TRM Copy Centers* Corp., 43 F.3d 29, 37 (2d Cir. 1994).

91 *Raza v. City of New York*, 998 F. Supp. at 83.

92 *Dinler v. City of New York*, 607 F.3d 923, 931 (2d Cir. 2010).

93 *Raza v. City of New York*, 998 F. Supp. at 82.
94 *Dinler v. City of New York*, 607 F.3d at 934–5.
95 *Raza v. City of New York*, 998 F. Supp. at 83–4, note 9.
96 Ibid. at 83.
97 Ibid.
98 Ibid.
99 Ibid. at 84.
100 Ibid.
101 Ibid., emphasis in original.
102 Ibid. at 84–5, emphasis in original.
103 Ibid. at 85–6.
104 Ibid. at 86.
105 *Pyke v. Cuomo*, 258 F.3d at 110.
106 *Raza v. New York*, 998 F. Supp. at 86.
107 Ibid. at 86–8.
108 Ibid. at 87.
109 Ibid.
110 Ibid. at 87–8.
111 Ibid. at 88.
112 Ibid.
113 Ibid. at 89.
114 Ludwik Fleck, *The Genesis and Development of a Scientific Fact* (Chicago: University of Chicago Press, 1979).
115 Carol Kaesuk Yoon, "Stephen Jay Gould, 60, Is Dead; Enlivened Evolutionary Theory," *The New York Times*, May 21, 2002, https://www.nytimes.com/2002/05/21/us/stephen-jay-gould-60-is-dead-enlivened-evolutionary-theory.html.
116 *See, e.g.*, Stephen Jay Gould, *Wonderful Life: The Burgess Shale and the Nature of History* (New York: W.W. Norton and Company, 1990), which examines the evolution of early life as recorded in the fossils of the Burgess Shale.

3

Countering "Jihadi Chic"

The Myth of the Jihadi Bride and the Yazidi Genocide

The romantic allure of being a jihadi bride, as described in Chapter 1, is just as important to de-mythologize in order to dismantle the mystique of jihadi cool. One of the most powerful counter-narratives to the glamour of jihadi cool/chic is the narrative of the Yazidi Genocide, which graphically illustrates the dark underside of being a jihadi bride, particularly if one is part of a group ISIS considers religiously "impure."

The term "genocide" is a highly politicized and historically freighted term because it triggers connotations of the Holocaust and gas chambers, and the contemporary imperative to intervene. However, its corollary counterpoint is the suppression of the possibility of diplomatic efforts that could quell mass abuses.[1] Nevertheless, as elaborated below, the case of the Yazidi persecution illustrates a clear example of when it is apt to use the term "genocide."

In June 2016, a UN Human Rights panel declared its finding that "[g]enocide has occurred and is ongoing" by ISIS against the Yazidi. Paulo Sergio Pinheiro, Chair of the Independent International Commission of Inquiry on Syria stated, in a press release statement issued by the UN High Commissioner for Human Rights (OHCHR) that "ISIS has subjected every Yazidi woman, child, or man that it has captured to the most horrific of atrocities."[2] The UN Commission's report made special mention of the thousands of women and girls still being held captive and being abused, often as slaves.[3]

The plight of the Yazidi has become much-publicized, resulting in a powerful international counter-narrative to the romanticized image presented by jihadi cool/chic. Amal Clooney, George Clooney's wife and renowned human rights lawyer, added celebrity power by agreeing to represent victims of the Yazidi genocide, including ISIS survivor and Nobel Peace Prize nominee, Nadia Murad.[4] Clooney expressed an intent to initiate an International Criminal Court investigation and eventually to seek prosecution of the various crimes committed against her client, Murad, and the Yazidi community.

Chapter 3, perhaps the most technically weighted, documents and examines the proliferation of media narratives about various Yazidi survivors, the majority of whom have been women, and the coverage of the Yazidi "Holocaust." The use of the term "Holocaust" in relation to the Yazidi genocide is particularly evocative, given its historical and documentary freightedness. Eventually, the chapter uses legal analysis and argumentation to clarify the collective traumatic narrative of the Yazidi genocide as a counterweight to the allure of the culture of jihadi cool/chic.

The Yazidi History of Persecution

Although Yazidi genealogy is obscure, they are believed to have descended from an ancient religion called the "Cult of Angels."[5] Of the three original branches of the Cult of Angels, only the Yazidis remain.[6] The Cult of Angels is the source of most non-Muslim faiths that the Kurds follow; although its origins are obscure, it appears to have absorbed many of the other religions around it.[7] Yazidism appears to be a blend of Mithraism, Mazdaism, and Zoroastrianism, along with elements of Christianity and Islam.[8] At its core is the belief in seven angelic beings/emanations who protect the universe, through whom a monotheistic God interacts with humankind.[9] However, their adoption of certain elements of Zoroastrianism, such as worship in a fire temple, and the unique worship of the fallen angel, Melek Tawwus, or Malek Taus, have led fanatical Muslims to brand them as devil worshippers.[10] This is because in Muslim culture, the name Melek is closely aligned with the name Shaytan, which is also the name for Satan in the Quran.[11] The association is made even stronger by the Yazidis' belief that it was Melek Taus, the peacock angel, who convinced Adam to leave the Garden of Eden; however, unlike the devil, Melek Taus's intent was to seek the greater good for Adam's welfare.[12] Furthermore, fanatical Muslims believe that the Cult is sexually promiscuous and shares their women at religious gatherings.[13] The Cult of Angels denies that this is true; nevertheless, the stereotype, and therefore, the group's persecution, persists.[14]

Although Yazidis have adopted some elements of Christianity and Islam, such as baptism and circumcision, they have generally remained faithful to their ancient traditions.[15] They have no official "Holy Book" but have two sacred texts: the Kitab el-Jelwa, or the Book of Revelation, and the Meshef Resh, or The Black Book.[16] Because they do not have a singular "Holy Book," their beliefs and traditions have been passed down orally.[17] Finally, Yazidis do not attempt to convert others and simply rely on recitation and bloodlines for the propagation of the faith.[18] Yazidis do not allow converts because they believe that if one does not respect one's own religion, one will not respect any other religion.[19] Additionally, Yazidism, being an ethno-religious faith, requires that its members not mix with non-Yazidis.[20] The Yazidi faith requires that a child have two Yazidi parents and strongly discourages mixed marriages.[21] It is precisely this resistance to assimilation by the dominant religions around them and, in particular, their recalcitrance to conversion to Islam that made Al-Qaeda declare them to be infidels, thus legitimizing ISIL's/ISIS's aggressive targeting of them.

The city of Sinjar in Northern Iraq used to be a haven for the Yazidis, not only because of its mountainous terrain but also because it had many of their holy sites and temples.[22] The group survived more than seventy-two massacres during the rule of the Ottoman Empire alone,[23] largely by retreating to the mountains when they were under siege or attack.[24] In addition to the strategic advantage of using the terrain, the Yazidis had a history of creating strong peaceful ties with other groups in the region, including the Muslim Kurds, with whom they had a "life-long obligation of mutual assistance and support."[25] "While intermarriage between the Yazidis and Arabs of Sinjar were rare, [there were] many friendships and working relationships across the two communities, underlining the nuanced nature of the relationships in Sinjar prior to the attack."[26] In terms of security, the Iraqi Kurdish forces, the Peshmerga, were in charge of bases and checkpoints throughout the Sinjar region; they were the only security force in the region at the time of the Yazidi massacre.[27]

The August 3, 2014, Attack

During the early hours of August 3, 2014, ISIS fighters emerged from their bases in Syria and Iraq and swept across Sinjar in Northwest Iraq, which was the home of the Yazidis.[28] The attack appeared well-organized, with its command center based in Mosul and a significant operational center in Tel Afar.[29] As they moved into Sinjar, the Peshmerga withdrew from their bases, failing to communicate the security situation to the local population; no evacuation orders were issued and most villages were unaware of the collapse of the security situation upon which they had come to rely.[30]

As word spread that the Peshmerga had abandoned their stations, a few ad hoc groups of lightly armed Yazidi men attempted to defend some villages, such as Girzerik and Siba Sheikh Khedir, trying to give their families and neighbors more time to escape.[31] By daybreak, Yazidi families from hundreds of villages across Sinjar were fleeing their homes in fear and panic, taking little with them; others were advised by their Arab neighbors to stay in the villages and raise white flags over their houses.[32] The fighters focused on capturing the fleeing Yazidis by setting up checkpoints and sending mobile patrols; within hours, Yazidis who had been unable to escape to the nearby city of Duhok were completely encircled by armed and black-clad ISIS fighters.[33] The Yazidis who had fled early enough to the upper plateau of Mount Sinjar found themselves trapped in temperatures rising above 50 degrees Celsius, with no access to food, water, and medical care.[34] On August 7, 2014, at the request of the Iraqi government, then US president Barack Obama announced American military intervention;[35] American, Iraqi, British, French, and Australian military forces airdropped water and other supplies to the Yazidis and attempted to evacuate the most vulnerable while the ISIS fighters shot at them.[36] Hundreds of Yazidis, including infants and young children, perished at Mount Sinjar before the Syrian Kurdish Forces, the People's Defense Units, together with Yazidi volunteers, were able to open and maintain a corridor between Syria and Mount Sinjar.[37]

Meanwhile, on lower ground, ISIS fighters captured thousands of Yazidis either in their villages or as they attempted to flee from August 3 through

August 5, 2014.[38] Almost all villages were emptied within seventy-two hours of the attack, with only Kocho village not being emptied until August 15, 2014. ISIS fighters then systematically separated the surviving Yazidis into three groups: men and boys aged approximately twelve and above;[39] women and children; and later, from the pool of male children who had been kept with the women, boys aged seven and above.[40]

ISIS Treatment of Yazidi Men and Boys Aged Approximately Twelve and Above

Following the separation of families, ISIS fighters summarily executed men and older boys who refused to convert to Islam, either by gunshots to the head or by slitting their throats, while their families were forced to watch.[41] Men from rural Yazidi villages who fled with personal firearms were immediately killed when their weapons were found.[42] Sometimes, ISIS fighters executed captured Yazidi men and boys just out of sight, but within hearing range, of the women and children; others tormented the women and children by telling them the lie that they had released the men and boys to escape to Mount Sinjar.[43]

The bodies of those immediately killed on capture were left in situ; captured Yazidis being forcibly transferred to Mosul and Tel Afar described being driven on roads, the sides of which were littered with corpses.[44] Most of the killings were done in small groups of two to twenty men and boys, but there were two clearly documented cases of larger mass killings in the Kocho and Qani villages.[45]

Men and boys who were forcibly "converted" to Islam became ISIS captives; they were transferred to work camps in Tel Afar, Mosul, and Baaj, where they were forced to work on construction projects, dig trenches, clean streets, and look after cattle.[46] They were also forced to pray, grow their beards and hair, and follow other religious dicta as promulgated by the terrorist group.[47]

ISIS recorded videos on their phones of "converted" Yazidi men and boys urging their relatives to convert, and these were shown to the men's families at holding sites in El Tafar and Badoush prison.[48] Families who converted were reunited in Qasr Maharab; widows and their children, if any, were moved to nearby Qasil Qio.[49] Later, ISIS would also forcibly transfer some "converted" families to the Al-Khadra neighborhood in El Tafar.[50]

All Yazidi men and boys were required to go to the mosque for prayers; nevertheless, "conversion" afforded them and their families no protection or equality in status.[51] Yazidis were not free to leave the villages and were subjected to regular counts.[52] Anyone who tried to escape was beaten on the first attempt and executed on the second.[53] When someone successfully escaped, members of their household were beaten.[54] Every day, ISIS took men and boys over twelve years of age out of the villages and forced them into slave labor in various cities and towns; anyone who refused to go was beaten.[55] ISIS fighters regularly seized unmarried women and girls and even married women who had no children. Despite the "conversions," ISIS fighters regularly continued to denigrate and insult the Yazidis held in Qasr Maharab, Qasil Qio, and Al-Khadra, calling them "kuffar" or infidels.[56] By the spring of 2015, ISIS determined that any "conversions" were deemed false, and in April or May 2015, ISIS emptied Qasr Maharab, Qasil Qio, and Al-Khadra, separating the families.[57]

ISIS Treatment of Yazidi Women and Girls Aged Nine and Above

After separating Yazidi women and children from their male relatives at least twelve years old, ISIS fighters proceeded to transfer them forcefully across a number of holding sites, starting with four to six sites in Iraq and eventually into Syria. The first holding site was usually the Sinjar region, where captives were held, on average, for less than twenty-four hours before they were transferred, unwillingly, to Tel Afar, Mosul, or Baaj.[58] For instance, women and children from Kocho and Qani villages were initially held at the Solagh Technical Institute (at different times), while those captured in the approximate vicinity of Sinjar town or in the area of Zalelah were held at the Civil Records Office or in Branch 17, KDP Headquarters inside Sinjar town.[59] In comparison, women and children from some villages on the north side of Mount Sinjar, including Khanasour and Sinouni villages, were transported to ISIS bases in Al-Hol and the Tel Hamis region in Hasakah, Syria, where they were registered before being coercively moved back into Iraq.[60]

At the primary holding sites, ISIS classified the Yazidi women and children into married females and unmarried females (presumed to be virgins); only girls aged eight years old or younger were allowed to remain with their mothers while boys were not separated from their mothers at this stage.[61] Adaptively intuiting that being placed in the "unmarried" category would subject them to the most danger, unmarried females or married females with no children immediately pretended their younger siblings or relatives were their biological children. However, there are some reports that members of Sinjar's Arab community provided assistance to ISIS by identifying those who were carrying on the subterfuge of being married.[62]

Occasionally, ISIS fighters registered captured Yazidi females at the primary holding sites; they recorded the Yazidi females' names, ages, the villages they came from, their marital status, and, if they were married, the number of children they had.[63] ISIS also took photos of the Yazidi females without their headscarves, with some being forced to smile and laugh while the photographs were being taken.[64] Such registration procedures were repeated in later holding sites in Tel Afar and Mosul, and for the women transported into Syria, again at the main holding location in Raqqah city.[65]

At the holding sites, the Yazidi females huddled together, trying to hide their adolescent daughters. ISIS fighters robbed the females of their valuables, including gold, money, and mobile telephones; as they did so, Yazidi women sought to write down or memorize phone numbers of relatives they hoped might be able to help them later.[66] There have also been reports of mass killings of older women. For example, during the early morning hours of August 16, 2014, ISIS executed women sixty years old or older from Kocho at the Solagh Technical Institute, where a mass grave has been discovered.[67]

Generally, ISIS held Yazidi women and children at primary holding sites for less than twenty-four hours before loading them onto trucks and buses and forcibly moving them to several secondary holding sites, such as multiple schools in Tel Afar; Badoush prison outside of Mosul city; Galaxy wedding hall in Mosul; as well as houses in the Al-Arabi neighborhood of Mosul city. Each Yazidi woman and child was held in one, and moved across two of three of these holding sites, which were operated by Iraqi ISIS fighters who used pseudonyms and supervised the forcible movement of the captives into Syria.[68]

As ISIS fighters purchased and transported women and girls, women and children were moved from site to site as space became available. Sometimes the move was due to security concerns. For example, in August 2014, Yazidi captives were suddenly moved from Badoush to schools in Tel Afar because a coalition airstrike struck a site in close proximity to the prison.[69]

Each holding site was severely overcrowded, holding hundreds and sometimes thousands of Yazidi women and children. Those held at secondary holding sites were given little food or water, with meager rations of food infested with insects, and the sources of water being toilets. No medical care was provided; at Badoush prison, a female gynecologist was given the assignment of identifying unmarried females who had lied about being married.[70]

Once Yazidi women and girls were at the holding sites, ISIS fighters came into the rooms where they were held, with the intent of selecting the females they wanted to take with them. The sound of footsteps in the corridor and of keys opening locks sent the women scurrying to the corners of the room, with mothers trying to hide their daughters. If any women tried to prevent the transfer of any girl, they were brutally beaten by the ISIS fighters.[71]

In an effort to render themselves unattractive to buyers, Yazidi females scratched and bloodied themselves. Suicide, or suicide attempts, were common. Some killed themselves by slitting their wrists or throats; others hung themselves using their head scarves. There was one reported instance in the main holding site of Raqqah city, where a Yazidi girl attempted to kill herself by jumping from the second floor of the building; ISIS fighters forbade the others from assisting the severely injured girl.[72]

Surprisingly, while individual incidents of rape were committed by ISIS fighters at the holding sites in Tel Afar and Mosul, there were no reports of mass rape, despite the fact that hundreds of women and girls were held captive at these sites, surrounded by dozens of young, armed men. This underlines the rigid ideology that underlay the system that treated Yazidi females as chattel and the control it had over its fighters. "The sexual violence, including sexual slavery, being committed against Yazidi women and girls [was] tightly controlled by ISIS, occur[ring] in a manner prescribed and authori[z]ed, and

[was] respectful only of the property rights of those who 'own[ed]' the women and girls."[73]

Captured Yazidi females were considered property of ISIS and openly called *sabaya* or slaves, and sold in slave markets or *souk sabaya* or in holding centers.[74] Based on a religious interpretation, ISIS made 80 percent of these females available to ISIS fighters for individual purchase.[75] Sometimes, much as a wholesaler does, an ISIS fighter could purchase a group of Yazidi females and sell them individually for higher prices in rural areas.[76] ISIS treated the remaining 20 percent as collective property and distributed them to military bases throughout Iraq and Syria, inclusive of, in particular, two locations in Raqqah city: an underground prison or security base and/or a group of buildings densely populated by trees, referred to by ISIS fighters as "the farm."[77]

Unmarried women and girls were sold quickly and immediately removed within a few days. However, others, such as women with more than three children, could remain in these holding sites for up to four months before they were sold.[78] Yazidi females were sold directly to fighters from the holding sites or slave markets; eventually, ISIS fighters started online slave auctions "using the encrypted Telegraph application to circulate photos of captured Yazidi women and girls, with details of their age, marital status, current location and price."[79] A central committee, the Committee for the Buying and Selling of Slaves, organized the Yazidi slave markets, and occasionally, delegated its functions to a local committee or commander.[80] An authenticated ISIS document explained that ISIS fighters had to preregister if they wished to attend a slave market in Homs, and specified that bids were to be submitted in sealed envelopes at the time of purchase, and those who won the bid were obligated to purchase the female slaves.[81] During slave auctions, Yazidi women, like livestock, were displayed in raised areas, or were forced to walk through the room like a catwalk, and their hair and teeth were examined; prices ranged from $200 to $1,500 depending on their marital status, age, number of children, and beauty, with the youngest ranging between seven and nine years old.[82] Buyers, or at least parties complicit with such slave auctions, seemed to come from all over the world, such as Iraq, Syria, Saudi Arabia, Turkey, Morocco, Algeria, Tunisia, Libya, Egypt, Kazakhstan, Sudan, Belgium, Uzbekistan, and Australia.[83] In keeping with general principles of contract law, once ISIS sold a Yazidi female, the purchasing fighter possessed complete ownership rights and could resell, gift, or bequeath her through a will as he desired.[84] And in keeping with general principles of property law, if a Yazidi slave's owner died intestate, she reverted back to the status of being "the collective property of ISIS, with the local Wali charged with organi[z]ing her resale."[85]

In Syria, Yazidi females (and any young children sold with their mothers) were kept locked in either the fighter's home, or alone in apartments and houses, or in makeshift shelters closer to the front lines or in gas fields.[86] Occasionally, fighters would bring Yazidi young boys with them to pray in the local mosque—a privilege not possible for Yazidi females who were not even given *abayas*[87] (loose fitting garments used to cover the body and head) and thus could easily be captured if they escaped because they were uncovered.[88]

ISIS fighters routinely and severely raped and beat Yazidi females over the age of nine, pregnant or not. To force compliance, some were threatened with the possibility of gang rape; of being thrown off a roof; of selling and beating their children. As if that were not enough, some were handcuffed behind their backs during the rapes, while others were spreadeagled, hands and feet tied to the corners of the beds. Wives and children of ISIS fighters sometimes participated in these beatings. The rapes resulted in "suffering, bleeding, cuts and bruising," and the Yazidi females and young children were denied access to medical care.[89] Resistance would simply lead to more severe beatings. Yazidi females and younger children were often resold several times. When escape attempts were thwarted, the consequences were dire; one woman reported that several of her children were killed, and she was repeatedly raped for six months afterward. Another scenario could be an organized gang rape and beating and reselling.[90]

Many Yazidi females reported being forced by their fighter-owners to take birth control, either in the form of pills or injections; however, there was no protection against sexually transmitted diseases. One Yazidi girl, who was eighteen at the time of her capture, was purchased by a Libyan fighter and held in an oil field compound in Dayr Az-Zawr; he raped her and forced her to take pills daily. She was held in captivity for a year, sold eight times, and raped hundreds of times, before she was resold to her family for over $20,000.[91]

Other women were not given any access to birth control. A woman bought by a Tunisian fighter was repeatedly raped in Al-Bab for several months without any form of birth control before she was sold to four different ISIS fighters prior to being smuggled out at an unknown cost to her family. However, her husband has since divorced her.[92]

Despite a general reticence regarding births that have resulted from such rapes, there have been reports of births in captivity or upon release; many of the Yazidi females appear to have given the infants away in circumstances that remain unclear.[93] ISIS fighters and sometimes their wives often also forced Yazidi females, in addition to being sex slaves, to be domestic servants: cooking food; babysitting or taking care of the ISIS fighter's children; washing clothes.[94] Nevertheless, Yazidi females and young children were denied adequate food and were additionally starved further after escape attempts. The verbal abuse of Yazidi females and young children was ubiquitous, with the object of insults being their faith, mistakenly alleging that they "worshipped stones" and that they were "dirty *kuffar*" and "devil-worshippers."[95]

ISIS had overarching rules regarding the resale of Yazidi females as *sabaya* ("spoils of war"). They were not supposed to be sold between brothers or until they had completed their menstrual cycles (thus indicating they were not pregnant). It was theoretically forbidden to sell them to non-ISIS members, and the punishment was death. However, all these rules were regularly breached by ISIS fighters, especially as the financial incentives to sell the Yazidi females and children back to their families were significant. "Whereas Yazidi women and children [were] sold between [$]200 and [$]1,500, they [were] generally sold back to their families for between [$]10,000 and [$]40,000."[96] Many of the families who bought back their relatives ended up being heavily in debt and worried about both making payments and having enough to buy back any other relatives that fighter-owners decided to sell in the future. Many continued to make payments to ISIS fighters, who regularly subjected them to threatening phone calls.[97]

Many of the Yazidi females interviewed bore physical wounds or scars from the abuse they endured; yet even more striking was the mental trauma from which all suffered. Many spoke of thoughts of suicide, being unable to sleep because of nightmares, and feeling angry and hopeless.[98] Women who were rescued or sold back tended to be consumed by thoughts of their missing relatives.[99] On a positive note, the Yazidi community has largely embraced the females who have returned from ISIS captivity, thus opening new cultural spaces that would allow them to marry and reintegrate back into society. Nevertheless, captured and released Yazidi females and children, in addition to the heavy physical and emotional toll, face a challenging future because of their limited education and their marrying young and having children, leaving them with little personal and financial independence.[100]

ISIS Treatment of Young Children Held with Their Mothers

ISIS sold Yazidi women and their children as a package deal. Once a Yazidi girl reached the age of nine, she was taken from her mother and sold as a slave. Once a Yazidi boy reached the age of seven, he was separated from his mother and sent to an ISIS training camp and from there on to battle. Younger siblings were witnesses to these separations, with their mothers being beaten as they tried to prevent the separation from the older siblings.[101]

ISIS fighters often targeted younger Yazidi children as a means of punishing their mothers, often killing them after a failed escape attempt. There is a report of a Yazidi woman being loaned to another ISIS fighter to be raped for one night, and her seven-year-old daughter subsequently raped in order to see if she "was ready to be married."[102] ISIS fighter-owners often beat children for making too much noise as their mothers were being separated from them or being raped, or for clinging to their mothers. Children and their mothers in captivity suffered the same poor living conditions, including lack of food and water, and in winter, sleeping in unheated rooms. ISIS fighters and their families routinely derided their Yazidi captives as "unclean"; some ISIS fighters forced Yazidi children to say the name of the devil aloud, which was impermissible in the Yazidi religion. Yazidi women in Internally Displaced People camps described their children as being unable to sleep and bed-wetting, flying into terrible rages, and suffering from anxiety when separated from their mothers, with especially the boys being highly protective of their mothers, particularly when unfamiliar men were present.[103]

ISIS Treatment of Yazidi Boys, Aged Seven and Above

ISIS permitted Yazidi boys who had not yet reached the age of puberty to remain for a time with their mothers and siblings. After the August 2014 attack, most boys and their mothers were moved to holding sites in Mosul and Tel Afar, where, if they were aged seven and above, they were separated from their families. Boys in families who had "converted" were transferred with their relatives to Qasr Maharab and Qasil Qio villages, where they were forced to attend prayers at local mosques and were severely beaten if they refused. " 'Converted' Yazidi boys were not taken for training until April or May 2015 when ISIS emptied the villages and separated the families."[104] Any mothers or siblings who tried to prevent the separation were severely beaten by the fighters, who made it clear that they were taking the young Yazidi males to train them as Muslims and as ISIS fighters ready to kill their own relatives.[105]

The separation of Yazidi boys who were seven years old and above was systematic. They were forcibly transferred to training centers or military camps in Mosul, Tel Afar, and Baaj in Iraq, and in Raqqah city, Tabqa, Tel Abyad, and Suluk in Syria.[106] Many training centers were set up in former schools, such as Mahad Farouq lil Ashbal in Tel Abyad.[107] There, the boys were registered, given Islamic names, and treated as new recruits.[108] ISIS fighters, acting as instructors, were in charge of indoctrination and military training sessions. Yazidi boys were mixed with Sunni Arab boys, who were also being trained, in groups of between ten and twelve. The daily routine consisted in sessions on Quranic recitation as well as military exercises, such as being taught to use AK47s, hand grenades, and Rocket Propelled Grenades.[109] The Yazidi boys were compelled to watch ISIS-produced propaganda videos of armed battles, beheadings, and suicide missions. Part of the indoctrination included sessions on "Jihad" and the significance of joining the war against "unbelievers." If the boys failed to memorize Quranic verses or performed poorly in training sessions, they were beaten.[110]

At the training centers or camps, all traces of the Yazidi boys' pasts were erased, and all contact with their family and community was cut off. New identities were forcibly enforced. There were thus two objectives to the indoctrination program. Generally, it was aimed at increasing recruitment;

more specifically, it was aimed at destroying the boys' identities as Yazidi and recasting them as ISIS followers of Islam. After completing the training, Yazidi boys were distributed according to the needs of the terrorist group.[111]

ISIS Destruction of Yazidi Temples and Shrines

As ISIS fighters conquered the Sinjar region in early August 2014, they began systematically destroying Yazidi temples and shrines. "The shrines of Sheikh Mand in Jiddala village, Sheikh Hassan in Gabara, Malak Fakhraddin in Sikeeniya, and Mahma Rasha located in Solagh were all destroyed in the period following the attack."[112] Additionally, after forcibly moving the Yazidis out of their homes, which the ISIS fighters marked with symbols that distinguished them from Arab houses, ISIS fighters looted these Yazidi homes and severely damaged or destroyed many of them.[113]

Legal Analysis

Genocide

Are the Yazidis a "protected group"?

Article II of the Genocide Convention, mirrored in Article 6 of the Rome Statute, characterizes a protected group as a "national, ethnic, racial, or religious group, as such."[114] The term "as such" signals that the prohibited act must be targeted based on an individual's membership in a specific group, and specifically because the individual belonged to the group, so the real victim is not merely the individual but more significantly, the group itself.[115]

The Yazidis are often described as an ethno-religious group.[116] Both ethnic and religious groups are protected groups as defined by Article II of the Genocide Convention, with ethnic groups described as groups "whose members share a common language or culture"[117] while religious groups are characterized as groups "whose members share the same religion, denomination or mode of worship."[118]

The question of whether the Yazidis constitute a distinct ethnic group is a matter of discussion within the group itself. Indigenous communities of Yazidis reside in Syria, Iraq, Armenia, and Turkey, and their native tongue is Kurdish.

With the exception of the Armenian Yazidis, many of these indigenous groups identify as Kurdish but followers of the Yazidi religion. "Where Yazidis hold the view of themselves an ethnically distinct group, this appears in the context of repression and discrimination against the Yazidi community by surrounding Muslim communities."[119]

In contrast, there is little debate regarding the Yazidis' identity as a distinct religious group. Yazidism is an indigenous religion that has existed for thousands of years but has absorbed some features of later faiths, notably Zoroastrianism, Judaism, Christianity, and Islam, while maintaining its unique traditions. "Without exception, diverse members of the Yazidi community interviewed were of the view that the Yazidis constitute a separate religious denomination, with distinct modes of worship."[120]

Additionally, jurisprudence from the International Criminal Tribunal for Rwanda (ICTR) and International Criminal Tribunal for the former Yugoslavia (ICTY) points out that the beliefs of the persecuting group may also be considered in determining membership of a protected group.[121] ISIS has consistently used the Yazidis' religious identity as the basis for its attack, persecution, and abuse, calling the Yazidis infidels and "dirty kuffar."[122] It is clear that ISIS does not consider Yazidism an immutable identity and has forced conversions; nevertheless, its later decision not to recognize any apparent "conversions" of Yazidi adults was spurred by the realization that these conversions were feigned. Nonetheless, ISIS continued to promote the indoctrination of younger Yazidi boys, forcing the boys to reject Yazidism and embrace, instead, ISIS ideology.[123] It is clear that the UN Commission "has, on the basis of objective and subjective definitions, determined the Yazidis are a protected religious group within the meaning of Article II of the Genocide Convention."[124]

Has ISIS committed one or more of the prohibited acts against members of the Yazidi group?

(a) Killing members of the group

ISIS intentionally slaughtered Yazidis as part of its attack on Sinjar. This includes Yazidis executed upon their capture, as well as the deaths that occurred as a result of ISIS's besieging of Yazidis who had retreated and become trapped on the mountain.[125] In August 2014, ISIS executed hundreds of Yazidi men and boys when they did not acquiesce to the demand that they convert to Islam or were found possessing weapons. Based on multiple eyewitness accounts, mass killings occurred in Kocho and Qani villages; the same conclusion can also be inferred from accounts of captured Yazidi women and young children who saw Yazidi men and adolescent boys led away by ISIS fighters, heard gunshots, saw the ISIS fighters covered with blood, and never again saw or heard from the Yazidi men and adolescent boys. In the early hours of August 16, 2014, an unknown number of older women from Kocho village were also summarily executed at the Solagh Technical Institute.[126] Based on a report from Yazda, there have been over thirty mass graves found in the Sinjar region, containing the remains of men and adolescent boys.[127]

Although most of the killing of Yazidis occurred in Iraq, ISIS fighters who had purchased Yazidi women and children also engaged in the murder of the captives. One account details how a Yazidi woman's attempt to escape failed, leading her Aleppo-based ISIS fighter-owner to kill several of her children, and when she wept, to beat the Yazidi woman for crying over the deaths of "kuffar children."[128]

Additionally, ICTY jurisprudence states that the suicide of an individual may amount to a killing where the defendant's acts or omissions "induced the victim to take actions which resulted in his death, and that his suicide was either intended, or was an action of a type which a reasonable person could have foreseen as a consequence."[129] Yazidi females, held in Syria and Iraq, and notably at the "farm" in Raqqah city, where they were gathered, registered, and sold, killed themselves before they could be sold to ISIS fighters.[130]

Clearly, therefore, as the UN Committee has found, ISIS has committed the prohibited act of killing members of a protected religious group, the Yazidis.[131]

(b) Causing serious bodily and/or mental harm to members of the group

Conduct that results in serious bodily and/or mental harm "may include, but is not necessarily restricted to, acts of torture, rape, sexual violence or inhuman or degrading treatment."[132] ICTR and ICTY jurisprudence has consistently held that such harm can mean torture, and inhuman and degrading treatment.[133] Additionally, such physical and/or mental harm need not rise to being permanent or irremediable.[134] As the facts above have demonstrated, ISIS has caused serious bodily and/or mental harm to the Yazidis.

(c) Rape and sexual violence, including sexual slavery

The ICTR case of *Akayesu* first found that rape and sexual violence comprise serious physical and mental harm, and therefore, if enacted with the specific intent to destroy, in whole or in part, a protected group, constitute genocide. As the findings of the Trial Chamber in the *Akayesu* case, hailed as "the most important decision rendered thus far in the history of women's jurisprudence,"[135] stated:

> Rape and sexual violence certainly constitute infliction of serious bodily and mental harm on the victims and are even, according to the Chamber, one of the worst ways of inflicting harm on the victim as he or she suffers both bodily and mental harm. . . . The rapes resulted in the physical and psychological destruction of the Tutsi women, their families and their communities. Sexual violence was an integral part of the process of destruction, specifically targeting Tutsi women and specifically contributing to their destruction and to the destruction of the Tutsi group as a whole.[136]

As documented above, ISIS fighter-owners systematically raped Yazidi females as young as nine years old. Beyond the individual rapes, Yazidi females, as a group, were subjected to entrenched sexual violence through sexual enslavement. Article 7(1) of the Rome Statute defines sexual slavery as a crime against humanity through the following material elements: (1) that the "perpetrator exercised any of all of the powers attaching to the right of ownership over one or more persons, such as purchasing, selling, lending or bartering such a person or persons, or by imposing on them a similar deprivation of liberty"[137] and (2) the "perpetrator caused such person or persons to engage in one or more acts of a sexual nature."[138]

The 2014 ICC (International Criminal Court) *Katanga* Trial Chamber Judgment held that "[p]owers attaching to right of ownership must be construed as the use, enjoyment, and disposal of a person who is regarded as property, by placing him or her in a situation of dependence which entails his or her deprivation of any form of autonomy."[139]

As the facts above show, once they were captured by ISIS, Yazidi females were deemed property of the terrorist group, and then later, of the individual fighters who bought them. After the August 2014 attack, Yazidi females were detained and registered in sites in Syria and Iraq, with the express purpose of determining their monetary value, thus effectively dehumanizing them. Subsequently, ISIS proceeded to organize sales of Yazidi females for individual fighters at holding sites, slave markets, and online auctions. Any attempts to refuse to be sold or to thwart efforts to sell other women were punished with violent beatings.[140]

Once they were sold, Yazidi females became the exclusive property of their fighter-owners, who could resell, lend, gift, or will them to other ISIS fighters. ISIS fighters threatened to kill Yazidi females who resisted rape, and also, in response to resistance, routinely beat and threatened any children Yazidi women had with them. ISIS fighters effectively blocked escape attempts by refusing to provide Yazidi females with any clothing, which would have allowed them to move unnoticed through the streets. Escape attempts were punished violently, inclusive of the killing of the Yazidi women's children, gang rape, rape, and beatings. Additionally, Yazidi females were forced into servile labor for the ISIS fighters and their families, cooking, cleaning, and washing clothes. Throughout their captivity, Yazidi females and children were treated as less than human and undeserving of respect and dignity because they were "dirty infidels."[141]

Captured Yazidi females immediately realized their absolute loss of any liberty; they had no choice over where they were taken, what happened to their children, to whom they were repeatedly sold, and how they were treated. An unknown number of Yazidi females, given such subjection to prolonged and brutal violence, committed or attempted to commit suicide. Captured females as young as nine were locked into houses or apartments, handcuffed and tied to beds, and raped. Many females were subjected to physical and psychological violence, including beatings and threats both to themselves and their children.[142]

Clearly, ISIS's sexual enslavement of Yazidi females was an act of sexual violence, initially set as a precedent in *Akayesu*, and followed in numerous ICTY and ICTR judgments, as "constituting serious bodily and mental harm within the meaning of Article II of the Genocide Convention."[143] Furthermore, it is clear from the aforementioned facts that the enslaved Yazidi females suffered serious physical and mental harm. Yet alongside the individual harms, it is also evident that these constitute a concerted "step in the process of destruction of the . . . group—destruction of the spirit, of the will to live, and of life itself."[144]

Nevertheless, Yazidi females were not only simply vessels for the destruction of the group; rape was not simply intended as a part of genocide but also was an individual attack against a female on the basis of her sex.[145] "The view of females as objects, not specific to ISIS, when backed by radical religious interpretation, and territorial control affording dominance over women and girls [found] a horrific, though logical, extreme in the terrorist group's conduct."[146] This was the common thread that connected how ISIS treated Sunni females, ordering them to be banished from the male gaze by remaining indoors or being fully covered when venturing out, and Yazidi females, as sex slaves. It is evident then, using an intersectional analysis, that Yazidi females were victimized both because of their sex and their religion.[147]

(d) Enslavement

Enslavement is a crime analytically distinct from sexual slavery. Enslavement is defined, as a crime against humanity, in Article 7(1)(c) of the Rome Statute and requires the defendant to have "exercised any or all of the powers attaching to the right of ownership over one or more persons, such as by purchasing, selling, lending or bartering such a person or persons, or by imposing on them a similar deprivation of liberty."[148] Relevant indicators of enslavement include "control of someone's movement, control of physical environment, psychological control, measures taken to prevent or deter escape, force, threat of force or coercion, duration, assertion of exclusivity, subjection to cruel treatment and abuse, control of sexuality and forced labour."[149]

ISIS fighter-owners compelled enslaved Yazidi females to perform domestic tasks, such as cooking, cleaning, and washing clothes for them and occasionally for their families. They were also forced to care for the fighter-owner's children and to assist the wife or the fighter-owner in keeping with any of their whims. Yazidi males over the age of puberty were similarly forced to work on construction and cleaning work, digging trenches, and looking after cattle in Tel Afar and Mosul.[150]

As recounted earlier, clearly ISIS fighters treated Yazidi females as chattel, bereft of dignity and autonomy, subjecting them to physical and psychological controls, including measures to prevent escape, and violent abuse as they trafficked the Yazidi females between Iraq and Syria. Yazidi males and females were subjected to forced labor, albeit in different environments, and any Yazidi who refused was subjected to severe beatings. Such acts were incremental steps in both destroying the individual and eradicating the group.[151]

(e) Torture and inhuman and degrading treatment

When they were captured, Yazidi women and young children suffered serious mental harm by being separated from their male relatives and being compelled to either bear witness to their murders or to watch them being taken away to an unknown fate.[152] As documented by survivor accounts, ISIS fighter-owners severely beat captured Yazidi females if they resisted rape, attempted to escape, refused to do assigned domestic tasks for the fighters and their families, or tried to prevent ISIS fighters from removing their children or siblings from their care. Yazidi mothers suffered all-consuming and unrelenting severe mental anguish as a result of their daughters being sold into sexual slavery and their sons being forcibly indoctrinated and recruited into ISIS forces. Both the sexual and physical violence, combined with severe mental trauma, which the Yazidi females over nine endured, rose to the level of torture, causing them serious physical and psychological harm.[153]

Yazidi females were treated as chattel, subject to registration and assessment of their monetary value at the holding sites. Sometimes, the registration process entailed forcing them to comply with being photographed without their headscarves and being forced to smile for the camera; at other times, they were forced to parade around without their headscarves for customers, who would make their selection. While in captivity, as is evident, Yazidi females were treated as bereft of human dignity and were continually told that they were "unclean" and "worship[ped] stones," thus subjecting them to inhuman and degrading treatment.[154]

Yazidi children were particularly vulnerable as they were subject to constant beating and maltreatment; while they were being so besieged, they were ever aware of the sexual violence perpetrated against their mothers, the threat of the impending separation from their older siblings, and the prospect of their being sold, while being constantly denigrated as "dirty infidels." These acts amount to torture and inhuman and degrading treatment, constituting grave bodily and mental harm.[155]

ISIS also caused serious physical and psychological harm to Yazidi boys who were over seven years of age through their violent and forced separation from their families, compelled conversions and corollary indoctrination, recruitment, military training (which included beatings, training on suicide bombing, watching violent war propaganda), and active participation in hostilities. All these abuses were aimed at eradicating the boys' identity as Yazidis.[156]

(f) Forcible transfer

ISIS forcibly transferred Yazidi males and females from the area of capture to different primary and then secondary holding sites in Syria and Iraq. ISIS, and after sales, individual fighters, forcibly transferred females and young children among multiple locations as they were continually sold and resold. Such forcible transfers caused serious mental harm to the victims that rises to constitute a prohibited act under Article II of the Genocide Convention and Article 6 of the Rome Statute.[157] It is clear that such violent transfers caused grave bodily and/or mental harm to the Yazidis, a protected religious group.[158]

(g) Deliberately inflicting on the group conditions of life calculated to bring about its physical destruction in whole or in part

This act of genocide outlines methods of destruction that do not immediately kill the targeted members of a group but are ultimately designed to seek their destruction.[159] The term "conditions of life" may include, though does not necessarily exhaust the phrase's meaning, the "deliberate deprivation of resources indispensable for survival, such as food or medical services, or systematic expulsion from homes."[160] Such a definition is in keeping with the established jurisprudence of the ICTR and ICTY.[161]

On August 3, 2014, ISIS surrounded and besieged Yazidis who had successfully retreated to the upper slopes of Mount Sinjar, cutting them off from food, water, and medical care, and isolating the victims in an environment where temperatures soared above 50 degrees Celsius. Additionally, ISIS fighters attacked planes attempting to drop water and food supplies, and helicopters which sought to rescue those in dire need of medical attention or were particularly vulnerable.[162]

In *Kayeshima*, the Trial Chamber determined that rape also constituted a method of destruction that does not "lead immediately to the death of members of the group."[163] In 2015, the International Court of Justice found that rape could fall within Article II(c) of the Genocide Convention, but cautioned that, in that particular case, "it has not been shown that these occurrences [of rape] were on such a scale to have amounted also to inflicting conditions of life on the group that were capable of bringing about its physical destruction in whole or in part."[164]

Yazidi females, captured by ISIS and multiply sold in Syria and Iraq, were subjected to organized sexual violence on a massive scale, with women and girls suffering multiple, sometimes hundreds, of rapes by various fighter-owners. In addition, captured Yazidi females and children, including infants, were allowed very little access to food, water, and medical care, and were severely beaten if they resisted or failed to obey orders. ISIS and its fighter-owners imposed these dire conditions in a calculated effort, progressively over time, to cause the deaths of Yazidi women and children. It is thus clear that ISIS committed the prohibited act of intentionally inflicting upon captured Yazidis conditions of life meant to bring about their destruction, in whole or in part.[165]

(h) Imposing measures intended to prevent births within the group

"Measures intended to prevent births within the group include rape; sexual mutilation; the practice of sterilisation; forced birth control; separation of the sexes; prohibition of marriages; impregnation of a woman to deprive group identity; and mental trauma resulting in a reluctance to procreate."[166] As has been documented, ISIS's first act, upon capture of the Yazidis, was to separate men and women and to assassinate hundreds of men (and older women); families were separated, with the momentary sole exception of the "converted" Yazidi men and their wives in Qasr Maharab. However, as mentioned above, in April or May 2015, ISIS emptied Qasr Maharab, and permanently separated Yazidi families at that time.[167]

The destructive effect on Yazidi families and society was particularly devastating because under Yazidi religious tradition, both parents had to be Yazidi in order for the child to be Yazidi, and conversions were not allowed. ISIS, through its pronouncements and acts, made it clear that it would not allow Yazidis to continue to exist as Yazidis in their territory. Through the acts of separating Yazidi men and women, killing hundreds of Yazidi men, and compelling conversions to Islam, ISIS imposed measures aimed at preventing births within the group.[168]

Rape can also be a measure to prevent births "when the person raped subsequently refuses to procreate, in the same way that members of a group can be led, through threats or trauma, not to procreate."[169] An expert in trauma psychology involved with the treatment of Yazidi females stated that there was a real anxiety around any contact with men and resultant sexual dysfunction; this was especially so for the younger girls, where rape was their first experience of sex and where the traumatic sexual violence occurred over an extended period of time at the hands of multiple men.[170] Hardly surprisingly, given this context, captured Yazidi females did not wish to contemplate marriage or even a relationship with men; furthermore, this was compounded by the belief that they had lost their honor, even if they had no choice in relation to the rapes. Thus, the rapes perpetrated by ISIS fighters on Yazidi females also constitute a measure to prevent births within the group.

(i) Forcibly transferring children of the group to another group

As described above, ISIS forcibly separated Yazidi children from their mothers along gender-based lines. Yazidi females, once they reached the age of nine, were sold as sex slaves to ISIS fighters in Syria and Iraq; Yazidi males, once they reached the age of seven, were dispatched to ISIS training bases in Syria and Iraq, where they were indoctrinated into Islam as ISIS interpreted it, and "converted" into ISIS fighters.[171] These physical separations from their mothers, initially achieved through brute physical force, removed the children not only from their community but also from the practice of their faith, and were intended to destroy the children's self-image as Yazidi. However, whereas Yazidi girls were suppressed from practicing their religion, Yazidi boys were thoroughly immersed in ISIS ideology. It is thus evident that ISIS engaged in the prohibited act of forcibly transferring Yazidi children to another group.[172]

Did ISIS commit the prohibited acts with the intent to destroy, in whole or in part, the Yazidis?

For a finding of genocide, it must be demonstrated that ISIS committed one of more of the prohibited acts outlined above, and listed in Article II of the Genocide Convention, and replicated in Article 6 of the Rome Statute, with the specific intent that these acts be aimed at the destruction, in whole or in part, of the Yazidis. As the ICTR Rutaganda Trial Judgment explained:

> For any of the acts charged to constitute genocide, the said acts must have been committed against one or more persons because such person or persons were members of a specific group, and specifically, because of their membership in this group. Thus, the victim is singled out not by reason of his individual identity, but rather on account on his being a member of a national, ethnical [*sic*], racial or religious group.[173]

Historically, this special intent to destroy has often been inferred from conduct, including statements. ISIS was very explicit that its targeting of Yazidis was motivated by its religious interpretation, and its public statements on this provided an invaluable source clearly illustrative of its specific intent.[174]

Genocidal intent may also be inferred from the defendant's "deeds and utterances considered together, as well as from the general context of the perpetration of other culpable acts systematically directed against the same group."[175] Pertinent conduct includes "the physical targeting of the group or their property, the use of derogatory language towards members of the targeted group, and the methodical way of planning."[176] Other factors from which genocidal intent could be inferred included, in this particular case, the scale of atrocities committed, their general nature, and the fact of specifically and systematically targeting individuals by virtue of their membership in a particular group, while excluding members of other groups.[177]

In its English-language magazine Dabiq, ISIS published an article entitled "The Revival of Slavery Before the Hour," which sought to determine, on religious grounds, how the Yazidis should be treated. In this article, ISIS declared: "Upon conquering the region of Sinjar . . . the Islamic State faced a population of Yazidis, a pagan minority existent for ages in the regions of Iraq and Sham [Syria]. Their continual existence to this day is a matter that Muslims should question as they will be asked about it on Judgment Day."[178]

> Once ISIS had decided that the Yazidis were a *mushrik* group, judged not to believe in God as worshipped by *Ahl Al-Kitab*, or the People of the Book, ISIS declared that it dealt with this group as the majority of *fuqaha* [religious scholars] have indicated how *mushrikin* should be dealt with. Unlike the Jews and the Christians, there was no room for the *jizyah* payment [a tax to be paid to avoid conversion or death]. Also their women could be enslaved unlike the female apostates who the majority of the *fuqaha* say cannot be enslaved and can only be given an ultimatum to repent or face the sword. After capture, the Yazidi women and children were then divided according to the Shariah [religious law] amongst the fighters of the Islamic State who participated in the Sinjar operations, after one fifth of the slaves were transferred to the Islamic State's authority to be divided as *khums* [spoils of war] . . . . The enslaved Yazidi families are now sold by the Islamic State soldiers as the mushrikin were sold by the Companions.[179]

It is thus clear that ISIS scholars' determination of the status of the Yazidi mandated how the ISIS fighters treated the Yazidi: ISIS's killing of the men and boys who did not convert; both its sexual enslavement and enslavement of Yazidi females; its violent abduction, indoctrination, and recruitment and conversion of Yazidi boys to be used in hostilities, all clearly flowed from ISIS's pronouncements.[180] Massive organizational efforts were exerted into aligning the ISIS fighters' treatment of the Yazidis and ISIS's ideological view of the targeted group; this involved the coordination of the nearly identical treatment of the Yazidis by the ISIS fighters who stormed Sinjar, the transfer of thousands of Yazidi captives to assigned primary and secondary holding sites, and the complex system of registering and selling Yazidi women and children.[181]

Furthermore, during and after the August 3, 2014 Sinjar attack, ISIS also destroyed Yazidi shrines and temples, as well as homes marked as Yazidi property. As the ICTY Appeals Chamber in the *Krstić* case held, "[t]he destruction of cultural property may serve evidentially to confirm an intent, to be gathered from other circumstances, to destroy the group, as such."[182] Personal motives, such as the desire for territorial control of the Sinjar region, or the sexual gratification from the sexual enslavement of Yazidi females, did not preclude the ISIS fighters having the specific intent to commit genocide.[183] It is evident that from the moment of first contact with the Yazidis, the group was targeted because they were Yazidis. Yazidi males were forced either to convert or die, both options leading to the extermination of their identities (or persons) as Yazidi. Mothers were told their sons would be trained to become Muslim, and sons were indoctrinated to kill their own family members if they remained Yazidi.[184] Only Yazidi females, some as young as nine years old, were held in ISIS military bases as sex slaves for ISIS fighters or sold as chattel in slave markets.[185]

The notion of ISIS's interpretation of Islam as a purifying force is echoed consistently in all of the ISIS fighters' interactions with the captured Yazidis, who were repeatedly told they were "dirty Yazidis" and "kuffar." The Dabiq article similarly stated: "Their creed is so deviant from the truth that even cross-worshipping Christians for ages considered them devil-worshippers and Satanists."[186]

No other religious group was as sorely discriminated against as the Yazidis. Arab villagers who chose not to flee were allowed to remain in their homes, and were not captured, killed, or enslaved. Although Christian communities living in ISIS-controlled territories lived difficult and precarious lives, as long as they paid the *jizya* tax, their right to exist as Christians was recognized.

In stark contrast, under ISIS's extreme interpretation of Islam, it was impermissible for the Yazidi to exist as Yazidi because they were not People of the Book.[187]

Both the public statements and conduct of ISIS clearly indicated the specific intent to destroy the Sinjar Yazidi group, which comprised the majority of the world's Yazidi population, in whole or in part.[188] There is sufficient and competent evidence to believe that ISIS committed prohibited acts, as outlined in Article II of the Genocide Convention and Article 6 of the Rome Statute, against individual Yazidis because of their identity as Yazidi, orchestrated as an incremental step in the overall objective of destroying the group. Thus, the UN Commission determined that ISIS committed prohibited acts with the specific intent to destroy, in whole or in part, the Yazidis of Sinjar, and therefore, committed genocide.[189]

Crimes Against Humanity

In its killing of the Yazidi population, ISIS committed the crime against humanity of murder and extermination. In its sexual enslavement, enslavement, and beating of Yazidi females, ISIS perpetrated crimes against humanity of sexual slavery, rape, sexual violence, enslavement, torture, other inhumane acts, and severe deprivation of liberty. By compelling Yazidi males to labor on ISIS projects, and beating them if they refused or resisted, ISIS committed crimes against humanity of enslavement, torture, and other inhumane acts. These crimes were committed based on ISIS's religious discrimination against the Yazidis, which also amounted to the crime against humanity of persecution.[190]

War Crimes

The facts show that the Yazidis, who were a civilian population not taking part in hostilities, were the principal target of the Sinjar invasion merely because ISIS considered them infidels. By orchestrating such an attack on the Yazidis, ISIS committed the war crime of attacking a civilian population.[191] Once ISIS had captured Sinjar, ISIS fighters proceeded to separate men and older boys from their female relatives and younger children, and then to execute those who refused to convert, often with their relatives witnessing these killings. ISIS did not hesitate to kill Yazidis, whether men, women, or children during their captivity in Iraq and Syria; such killings constituted the war crime of murder.[192] The brutal acts of sexual violence that the Yazidi females endured took place within the context of an armed conflict and therefore were war crimes. In addition to the individual rapes, Yazidi females were deprived of their liberty and repeatedly sold, as property, for the purpose of being sexually abused; thus, ISIS committed the war crimes of rape, sexual violence, and sexual slavery.[193]

The treatment that the Yazidi females endured while in captivity effectively stripped them of their dignity and caused them indescribable physical pain and mental suffering; they were violently and regularly raped, often by different men and over a prolonged period of time, as well as beaten, sold as chattel, insulted, and humiliated. These experiences left incurable psychological scars on survivors. By deliberately inflicting severe pain and suffering on the Yazidi civilian females, ISIS committed the war crimes of torture, cruel treatment, and outrages upon personal liberty.[194] In relation to ISIS's abuse of Yazidi boys between the ages of seven and fifteen, ISIS committed the war crime of using, conscripting, and enlisting children.[195] ISIS clearly systematically separated the Yazidi boys from their mothers, forcibly training them, and then deploying them in armed hostilities in Syria.[196]

Human Rights Abuses

In addition to the aforementioned crimes of genocide, crimes against humanity, and war crimes, the underlying acts against the Yazidis described above constituted, in and of themselves, serious violations of international human rights law. Examples included violations of the right to life, liberty, and security of the individual; the proscription against torture and other cruel and inhumane acts; the freedom of religion or belief; and the prohibition against slavery. The forced displacement and multiple resale of females rose to human trafficking. The fate of thousands of males remains unknown and comprised the crime of enforced disappearance.[197]

Conclusions

Far from the glamorous depictions of jihadi cool and its feminine counterpart, jihadi chic, a fact-based and legally grounded analysis of the Yazidi Holocaust reveals a stark narrative of genocide, multiple crimes against humanity, and war crimes against a protected religious group, the Yazidis. This chapter offers a detailed account of the genocide perpetrated by ISIS on the Yazidi people, as well as the ideological grounds that motivated and justified such a gruesome and systematic destruction. The genocide against the Yazidis was perpetrated less through mass murder, though mass exterminations of Yazidi males and females did occur. Rather, ISIS sought to destroy the Yazidis in multiple, orchestrated ways inclusive of executions, sexual slavery, enslavement, torture and inhuman and degrading treatment, and forcible transfer resulting in serious bodily and mental harm. As part of this program of systematic eradication, ISIS imposed conditions of life that resulted in slow deaths; enforced measures to prevent Yazidi children from being born, inclusive of the forced conversion of adults, the separation of Yazidi men and women, and mental trauma. Additionally, ISIS transferred Yazidi children from their own families and relocated them with ISIS fighters, whose indoctrination and subjugation cut them off from the beliefs and practices of their own religious group, with the objective of eradicating their identities as Yazidis. Very clearly, ISIS's public statements and its conduct illustrated that ISIS had the specific intent to destroy the Yazidis of Sinjar, in whole or in part.

Hardly uniquely, this genocidal intent was buttressed by the warped belief that the world, as ISIS understood it, would be rendered a more "perfect" and "purer" place through the destruction of, in ISIS's view, the offending "dirty infidels." ISIS committed the crime of genocide against individual Yazidis as part of the larger program of destroying this religious community. "This [was] the genocide accomplished through the destruction of a nine-year-old girl in a slave market, surrounded by men waving their bids; of a woman and children locked in a room, beaten and starved; of a little boy trained to kill his father."[198] It was a genocide perpetrated by not only ISIS fighter-owners but also their families, who were all so ironically ideologically enslaved that they believed that by committing some of the most terrible crimes imaginable, they were improving the society in which they lived. This detailed analysis of the ideological grounds that motivated and justified such a gruesome and systematic destruction, using international law (as juxtaposed with US Constitutional and case law in Chapter 2), is a necessary building block for the final chapter, which engages the act of witnessing from an ethical perspective.

Notes

1 For an analysis of the strategic value of using the term "crime against humanity," as opposed to "genocide," see Tasnim Motala, "The Genocide Name Game: The Case for Crimes Against Humanity to Prevent Genocide," *Quinnipiac Law Review* 37 (2019): 611.

2 "UN Human Rights Panel Concludes ISIL Is Committing Genocide Against Yazidis," *UN News Centre*, June 16, 2016.

3 "'They Came To Destroy': ISIS Crimes Against the Yazidis," *U.N. Human Rights Council*, Thirty-second session, Agenda Item 4, Human Rights Situations that Require the Council's Attention, June 15, 2016, https://www.ohchr.org/sites/default/files/Documents/HRBodies/HRCouncil/CoISyria/A_HRC_32_CRP.2_en.pdf.

4 Lucy Westcott, "Amal Clooney Says U.N. has Failed Yazidi Women," *Newsweek*, September 17, 2016.

5 Reid C. Pizler, "Essay: Peace is not the Absence of Conflict, but the Presence of Justice," *NIU Law Review* 29, no. 2 (2009): 335, 361 (recounting Yazidi history).

6 Kurdistanica.com, "Cult of Angels," 2008, accessed January 5, 2014, http://www.kurdistanica.com/?qde/101 (explaining an ancient religion known as the Cult of Angels).

7 Ibid.

8 Pizler, "Essay: Peace is not the Absence of Conflict, but the Presence of Justice," 335, 362; Raya Jalabi, "Who Are the Yazidis and Why is ISIS Hunting Them?," *The Guardian*, August 11, 2014, https://www.theguardian.com/world/2014/aug/07/who-yazidi-isis-iraq-religion-ethnicity-mountains (describing Yazidi history including genocides as recent as 2007). See also "Mithraism,"

Encyclopedia Britannica, accessed March 3, 2024, https://www.britannica.com/topic/Mithraism (defining Mithraism). Mithraism is a polytheistic, pagan pre-Zoroastrian religion whose fulcrum is based on the worship of the Iranian god Mithra, the god of "sun, justice, contract and war." Ibid. This religion was based on loyalty to the emperor and was widely followed until Emperor Constantine accepted Christianity. Ibid. Philosophers denounced the "heathen aspects" of Mithraism and created the Zoroastrian religion, transforming it into a monotheistic religion, focused on the worship of one god, Mithra, the god of the sun. Ibid. See also "Mazdaism," *The Free Dictionary*, accessed March 3, 2024, https://www.thefreedictionary.com/Mazdaism (defining Mazdaism). Mazdaism is also an ancient Iranian religion focused on Ahura Mazda as the "source of all light and good." Ibid. Contemporary scholars use the term Mazdaism interchangeably with Zoroastrianism. Ibid. See also British Broad. Corp., "Zoroastrianism at a Glance," *Zoroastrianism*, 2009, accessed October 2, 2009, https://www.bbc.co.uk/religion/religions/zoroastrian/ataglance/glance.shtml (summarizing the history of Zoroastrianism). Drawing from Zoroastrianism, Yazidis worship collectively in a fire temple as they believe the worship of fire is a "manifestation from God," that the elements are pure, and that fire in particular reflects God's light or wisdom. Ibid. The Cult of Angels believes in the social equality of all people. Kurdistanica.com, "Cult of Angels." From Hinduism, the Yazidi adopt the belief in the reincarnation of souls; they believe that both good and evil are "equally important and fundamental to the creation and continuation of the material world." Ibid. They do not believe in a physical heaven and hell, but they firmly believe that good and evil from heaven and hell occur in the world and through the reincarnation of their followers. Ibid. Like several religions, they believe in a judgment day that shall occur at the end of time. Ibid.

9 Kurdistanica.com, "Cult of Angels."

10 Pizler, "Essay: Peace is not the Absence of Conflict, but the Presence of Justice," 335, 366.

11 Ibid. at 366.

12 ReligionForBreakfast, "Yazidi Religion Explained," YouTube video, September 10, 2020, https://www.youtube.com/watch?v=QRB9e9Ol4Hs.

13 Kurdistanica.com, "Cult of Angels."

14 Ibid.

15 Jalabi, "Who Are the Yazidis and Why is ISIS Hunting Them?"

16 Pizler, "Essay: Peace is not the Absence of Conflict, but the Presence of Justice," 335, 366.

17 Ibid. at 365; "Why did Isis Attack the Yezidi People?," *CBS News*, May 8, 2016, 6:35 PM, https://www.cbsnews.com/news/60-minutes-overtime-why-did-isis-attack-the-yezidi-people/.

18 Pizler, "Essay: Peace is not the Absence of Conflict, but the Presence of Justice," 335, 365; Kurdistanica.com, "Cult of Angels."

19 Pizler, "Essay: Peace is not the Absence of Conflict, but the Presence of Justice," 335, 365.

20 Sarah A. Johns, "The Long Term-Failings of Internally Displaced Person Status: A Case Study of the Ĕzidi People," *Notre Dame Journal of International and Comparative Law* 13, no. 2 (2023): 39–57.

21 "'They Came to Destroy': ISIS Crimes Against the Yazidis," 6.

22 Johns, "The Long Term-failings of Internally Displaced Persons," 42.

23 Jalabi, "Who Are the Yazidis and Why is ISIS Hunting Them?"; see also Simon Tomlinson and Tom McTague, "'ISIS Want to Impregnate Yazidi Women and Smash Our Bloodline': Fears Grow for the 300 Women Kidnapped from Sinjar," *MailOnline*, August 14, 2014, https://www.dailymail.co.uk/news/article-2724658/Were-not-leaving-Yazidis-refusing-come-mountain-300-women-stolen-ISIS-impregnated-smash-blond-bloodline.html. "Successive Waves of Persecution—they Claim to have Survived 72 Genocides—by the Ottoman Turkish Rulers of What is Now Iraq, by Saddam Hussein and now by Islamic Militants, have Reduced the Number of Yazidis from Millions to an Estimated 700,000." Ibid.

24 Pizler, "Essay: Peace is not the Absence of Conflict, but the Presence of Justice," 335, 366. The Yazidis have consistently preferred to erect their shelters and shrines in mountainous terrain because of the "unique defense mechanism" the terrain affords. Ibid.

25 Ibid. at 366.

26 "'They Came to Destroy': ISIS Crimes Against the Yazidis," 6.

27 Ibid.

28 Ibid. at 3.

29 Ibid. at 6.

30 Ibid. at 7.

31 Ibid.

32 Ibid.

33 Ibid.

34 Ibid.

35 The White House, *Statement by the President*, August 7, 2014, https://obamawhitehouse.archives.gov/the-press-office/2014/08/07/statement-president.

36 "'They Came to Destroy': ISIS Crimes Against the Yazidis," 7.

37 Ibid.

38 Ibid. See also A/HRC/28/18, para 19 and the US Holocaust Memorial Museum Report, pp. 18–19. Ibid. at n. 13.

39 The determination of whether boys had reached puberty occurred using various ways: fighters in Kocho village inspected Yazidi boys to see if they had underarm hair; others made snap judgments based on height and weight. Ibid. n. 12.

40 Ibid. at 8.

41 Ibid.

42 Ibid.

43 Ibid.

44 Ibid.

45 Ibid.

46 Ibid. at 9.

47 Ibid.

48 Ibid.

49 Ibid.

50 Ibid.

51 Ibid.

52 Ibid.

53 Ibid.

54 Ibid.

55 Ibid.

56 Ibid.

57 Ibid.

58 Ibid. at 10.

59 Ibid.

60 Ibid.

61 Ibid.

62 Ibid.

63 Ibid.

64 Ibid. at 11.

65 Ibid.

66 Ibid.

67 Ibid.

68 Ibid.

69 Ibid.

70 Ibid.

71 Ibid. at 11–12.

72 Ibid. at 12.

73 Ibid.

74 Ibid.

75 Ibid.

76 Ibid.

77 Ibid.

78 Ibid.

79 Ibid.

80 Ibid. at 13.

81 Ibid. (citing trans. Aymenn Jawad Al-Tamimi, http://www.aymennjawad.org/2016/01/archive-of-islamic-state-administrative-documents-1).

82 Ibid.

83 Ibid.

84 Ibid.

85 Ibid. at 13–14.

86 Ibid. at 14.

87 Ibid.

88 Ibid.

89 Ibid.

90 Ibid.

91 Ibid. at 15.

92 Ibid.

93 Ibid.

94 Ibid.

95 Ibid.

96 Ibid.

97 Ibid. at 15–16.

98 Ibid. at 16.

99 Ibid.

100 Ibid.

101 Ibid. at 17.
102 Ibid.
103 Ibid.
104 Ibid.
105 Ibid. at 18.
106 Ibid. at 19.
107 Ibid.
108 Ibid.
109 Ibid.
110 Ibid.
111 Ibid.
112 Ibid.
113 Ibid.
114 Ibid. at 20.
115 Ibid., citing Prosecutor v. Muhimana, ICTR Trial Judgment, April 28, 2005 ("Muhimana Trial Judgment"), para. 500; Prosecutor v. Kajelijeli, ICTR Trial Judgment, December 1, 2003 ("Kajelijeli Trial Judgment"), para. 813.
116 Ibid., referencing UNHCR's Eligibility Guidelines for Assessing the International Protection Needs of Iraqi Asylum Seekers.
117 Ibid., citing Prosecutor v. Akayesu, ICTR Trial Judgment, September 2, 1998 ("Akayesu Trial Judgment"), para. 513.
118 Ibid., citing Akayesu Trial Judgment, para. 515.
119 Ibid.
120 Ibid.
121 Ibid., citing Prosecutor v. Stakić, ICTY Appeals Judgment, July 31, 2003, para. 25; Prosecutor v. Gacumbitsi, ICTR Trial Judgment, June 17, 2004 ("Gacumbitsi Trial Judgment"), para. 255; Prosecutor v. Musema, ICTR Trial Judgment, January 27, 2000 ("Musema Trial Judgment"), para. 161.
122 Ibid.
123 Ibid. at 20–1.
124 Ibid. at 21.
125 Ibid., citing Akayesu Trial Judgment, para. 589, for the material elements of the act of killing.
126 Ibid.
127 Ibid., citing Yazda Mass Graves Report, pp. 7–20.
128 Ibid.

129 Ibid., citing Prosecutor v. Krnojelac, ICTY Trial Judgment, March 15, 2002, para. 329.

130 Ibid.

131 Ibid.

132 Ibid. at 22, citing Footnote 3 of Article 6(b) of the Rome Statute.

133 Ibid., citing Akayesu Trial Judgment, para. 504; Prosecutor v. Krstić, ICTY Trial Judgment, August 2, 2001, ("Krstić Trial Judgment"), para. 513; Prosecutor v. Karadžić et al., Review of the Indictment Pursuant to Rule 61 of the Rules of Procedure and Evidence, July 11, 1996, para. 93.

134 Ibid., citing Akayesu Trial Judgment, para. 502.

135 Ibid., citing Kelly Askin, Women's Issues in International Criminal Law: Recent Developments and the Potential Contribution of the ICC, in International Crimes, Peace and Human Rights: The Role of the International Criminal Court 47, 52 (Dinah Shelton ed., 2000).

136 Ibid., citing Akayesu Trial Judgment, para. 731. See also similar findings that rape and sexual violence were acts of genocide in Prosecutor v. Stakić, Trial Judgment, July 31, 2003 ("Stakić Trial Judgment") para. 516; Prosecutor v. Rutaganda, ICTR Trial Judgment, December 6, 1999 ("Rutaganda Trial Judgment"), para. 51; Musema Trial Judgment, para. 156; Gacumbitsi Trial Judgment, paras. 291–2; and Muhimana Trial Judgment, para. 502.

137 Ibid. at 22–3, citing Footnote 18 of Art. 7(1)(g), Rome Statute, which reads: "It is understood that such deprivation of liberty may, in some circumstances, include exacting forced labour or otherwise reducing a person to a servile status as defined in the Supplementary Convention on the Abolition of Slavery, the Slave Trade, and Institutions and Practices Similar to Slavery of 1956. It is also understood that the conduct described in this element includes trafficking in persons, in particular women and children."

138 Ibid. at 23.

139 Ibid., citing Prosecutor v. Katanga, ICC Trial Judgment, March 7, 2014 ("Katanga Trial Judgment"), para. 975 and para. 977, which listed the following non-exhaustive objective factors: "detention or captivity and their respective duration; restrictions on freedom to come and go or on any freedom of choice or movement; and, more generally, any measure taken to prevent or deter any attempt at escape. The use of threats, force or other forms of physical or mental coercion, the exaction of forced labour, the exertion of psychological pressure, the victim's vulnerability and the socioeconomic conditions in which the pow

is exerted may also be taken into account." Nevertheless, in its analysis of the first constituent element of the crime, the Trial Chamber stated that it would also take subjective factors into consideration, namely, "the person's perception of his or her situation as well as his or her reasonable fear." Furthermore, the Trial Chamber said that the second element of the crime involves "the victim's ability to decide the conditions in which he or she engages in sexual activity."

140 Ibid.

141 Ibid.

142 Ibid. at 23–4, referencing Cécile Aptel, "Child Slaves and Child Brides," *Journal of International Criminal Justice* 14, no. 2 (2016): 1–21.

143 Ibid. at 24.

144 Ibid., citing Akayesu Trial Judgment, para. 732 and Catharine A. McKinnon, "Rape, Genocide, and Women's Human Rights," *Harvard Women's Law Journal* 17, no. 5 (1994): 11–12, which states, in relevant part: "It is a rape to drive a wedge through a community, to shatter a society, to destroy a people. It is rape as genocide."

145 Ibid., citing Beth Van Schaak, "Engendering Genocide: The Akayesu Case Before the International Criminal Tribunal for Rwanda," Santa Clara University School of Law, Legal Studies Research Paper Series, July 2008, and Sherrie L. Russell-Brown, "Rape as an Act of Genocide," *Berkeley Journal of International Law* 21, no. 2 (2003): 350–74.

146 Ibid.

147 An intersectional analysis takes into account how race, gender, and class, for example, are not isolated indicia of personhood and privilege, but operate as concrete foundations of power, which interact much like variables. See Kimberle Crenshaw, "Mapping the Margins: Intersectionality, Identity Politics, and Violence against Women of Color," in *Critical Race Theory: The Key Writings that Formed the Movement*, ed. Kimberle Crenshaw, Neil Gotanda, Gary Peller, and Kendall Thomas (New York: The New York Press, 1995), 357–83.

148 "'They Came to Destroy': ISIS Crimes Against the Yazidis," 3 citing Footnote 11 attached to Article 7(1)(c), Rome Statute which states: "It is understood that such deprivation of liberty may, in some circumstances, include exacting forced labour or otherwise reducing a person to a servile status as defined in the Supplementary Convention on the Abolition of Slavery, the Slave Trade, and Institutions and Practices Similar to Slavery of 1956. It is also understood

that the conduct described in this element includes trafficking in persons, in particular women and children."

149 Ibid. at 24–5, citing Prosecutor v. Kunarac, ICTY Trial Judgment, February 22, 2001, para. 542; confirmed in Prosecutor v. Kunarac, ICTY Appeals Judgment, June 12, 2002, para. 119; later followed in Prosecutor v. Kaing (alias Duch), ECCC Trial Judgment, July 26, 2010, para. 342; and the 2012 Taylor Trial Judgment, para. 447. Caveat: the ICTY Statute, unlike the ICC Statute, did not contain the separate crime of sexual slavery as distinct from slavery.

150 Ibid. at 25.

151 Ibid.

152 Ibid., citing Prosecutor v. Tolimir, ICTY Trial Judgment, December 12, 2012, para. 756; Prosecutor v. Karadžić, ICTY Trial Judgment, March 24, 2016, ("Karadžić Trial Judgment") para. 6049.

153 Ibid.

154 Ibid. at 25–6.

155 Ibid. at 26.

156 Ibid.

157 Ibid., citing Prosecutor v. Tolimir, ICTY Appeals Judgment, April 8, 2015, para. 209, and Karadžić Trial Judgment, para. 545.

158 Ibid.

159 Ibid., citing Akayesu Trial Judgment, para. 505.

160 Ibid., citing Footnote 4, Article 6(c) of the Rome Statute.

161 Ibid., citing, for example, Akayesu Trial Judgment, para. 506; Rutaganda Trial Judgment, para. 52; Musema Trial Judgment, para. 157; Stakić Trial Judgment, para. 517.

162 Ibid.

163 Ibid. at 27, citing Prosecutor v. Kayishema et al., ICTR Trial Judgment, May 21, 1999 ("Kayishema Trial Judgment"), para. 116.

164 Ibid., citing Republic of Croatia v. Republic of Serbia, Application of the Convention on the Prevention and Punishment of the Crime of Genocide, ICJ Judgment, February 3, 2015, paras. 362–4.

165 Ibid.

166 Ibid., citing Akayesu Trial Judgment, paras. 507–8 and Rutaganda Trial Judgment, para. 53.

167 Ibid.

168 Ibid.

169 Ibid., citing Akayesu Trial Judgment, para. 508.

170 Ibid. at 27–8.

171 Ibid. at 28.

172 Ibid.

173 Ibid., citing Rutaganda Trial Judgment, para. 60.

174 Ibid.

175 Ibid. at 29, citing Gacumbitsi Trial Judgment, para. 252.

176 Ibid., citing Kayishema Trial Judgment, para. 93.

177 Ibid., citing Akayesu Trial Judgment, para. 523; Kajelijeli Trial Judgment, paras. 804–5.

178 Ibid., citing Dabiq, "The Revival of Slavery Before the Hour," *Dabiq* 4 (2014): 14–16 ("Dabiq article"); see p. 14, which stated that prior to the conquest of Sinjar, Shari'ah students in the Islamic State were organized to research the Yazidi group to analyze whether they should be treated as an originally mushrik group or were originally Muslim and subsequently apostatized.

179 Ibid., citing Dabiq article at 15, unless otherwise indicated, in general, the emphasis was in the original.

180 Ibid., citing, for example, "Unseen Islamic State Pamphlet on Slavery," trans. Aymenn Jawad Al-Tamimi (http://www.aymennjawad.org/2015/12/unseen-islamic-state-pamphlet-on-slavery).

181 Ibid. at 30.

182 Ibid., citing Prosecutor v. Krstić, ICTY Appeals Judgment, April 19, 2014, para. 25–26. See especially para. 580 of the Krstić Trial Judgment, which stated: "Where there is physical or biological destruction there are often simultaneous attacks on the cultural and religious property and symbols of the targeted group as well, attacks which may legitimately be considered as evidence of intent to physically destroy the group. In this case, the Trial Chamber will thus take into account as evidence of intent to destroy the group, the deliberate destruction of mosques and houses belonging to members of the group." See also Bosnia and Herzegovina v. Serbia and Montenegro, Application of the Convention on the Prevention and Punishment of the Crime of Genocide, ICJ (International Court of Justice) Judgment, February 26, 2006 ("Bosnia v. Serbia Judgment"), para. 344.

183 Ibid., citing Prosecutor v. Jelisić, ICTY Appeals Judgment, July 5, 2001, para. 49.

184 Ibid.

185 Ibid.

186 Ibid., citing Dabiq article at 14.

187 Ibid. at 30–1.

188 Ibid. at 31, citing Kayishema Trial Judgment, para. 96; Krstić Trial Judgment, para. 590.

189 Ibid., citing Jelisić Trial Judgment, para. 66.

190 Ibid., citing Prosecutor v. Tadic ICTY Trial Judgment, May 7, 1977, paras. 704–10; Prosecutor v. Kupreskić, ICTY Trial Judgment, January 14, 2000, para. 594.

191 Ibid. at 32.

192 Ibid.

193 Ibid.

194 Ibid.

195 Ibid., noting that "[u]nder the 2002 Optional Protocol to the Convention on the Rights of the Child on the involvement of children in armed conflict, non-state armed groups, such as ISIS, are precluded from the recruitment and use of children under the age of eighteen. Syria ratified the Optional Protocol in 2003."

196 Ibid.

197 Ibid.

198 Ibid. at 36–7.

4

Toward a Poethics of Witnessing

Chapter 1 analyzed the rhetorical and aesthetic dynamics of a culture of jihadi cool/chic, and why these rhetorical and aesthetic techniques have been such a powerful recruitment force for particular terrorist groups. Crucial to this analysis is the distinction between radicalization of thought and radicalization of action because a theoretical rhetoric of radicalization does not automatically convert into a rhetoric of radical action unless there are catalysts at work. The internet, as well as imagined relations cemented by the rhetorics of jihadi cool or chic, can function as crucial catalysts, galvanizing monster talk into monstrous action.[1] Of course, this insight always needs to be nuanced with the empirically based finding by various terrorism experts that there is no single deterministic pathway toward radicalization. For example, former CIA officer and psychologist, Marc Sageman, analyzed over 500 cases to arrive at the insight that although one could describe distinct stages of radicalization,[2] he cautioned against the illusion that "[o]ne can simply draw a line, put markers on it and gauge where people are along this path to see whether they are close to committing atrocities."[3] Similarly, the Rand Corporation, based on a fourteen-year study of the process of radicalization, concluded that "no single pathway towards terrorism exists"[4] and that the attempt to predict who, among a group of similarly situated individuals, would likely adopt radical views, much less turn violent, is fraught with difficulty, as much seems to be due to "happenstance."[5] Finally, in a Department of Homeland Security-supported study, Clark McCauley and Sophia Moskalenko concluded that although they had outlined twelve possible pathways to radicalization (while leaving room for the possible discovery of more), that "radicalization progression cannot be understood as an invariable set of steps or 'stages' from sympathy to radicalism."[6]

Crucial to the appeal of jihadi cool/chic are the ability to communicate in the American vernacular in a manner that appeals to the youth, as well as a command of what it takes to create what used to be cognizable as an MTV aesthetic, as significant components of jihadi cool's rhetorical persuasiveness. Videos created specifically for Western audiences try to depict jihad as a "Hollywood-like video game."[7] Yet despite this imagined appeal to the virtual worlds of Hollywood video and MTV aesthetics, these "jihadi cool" videos attempt a connection to "reality" by humanizing the radical jihadi warriors. Hence, radical jihadi warriors are shown with cats and dogs,[8] and with American products that would appeal to their young audiences, such as Nutella, a chocolate spread, and Skittles, a rainbow-like colorful candy.[9]

Furthermore, as illustrated above, jihadi cool/chic videos are micro-tailored to draw in different and particularly targeted audiences. Indeed, there has been much recent research analyzing the Islamic State's micro-tailoring of its messages so as to appeal to particular audiences, similar to the way marketing companies aim their ads to cater to the preferences, values, and "likes" of particular groups.[10] Some of jihadi cool's/chic's appeal lies in its ability to tap into the fantasies of the young, which are also gendered in a conservative manner: for young men, for example, the glory of being a warrior and the thrill of adventures on the battlefield, and the promise of unyielding brotherhood are compelling;[11] for young women, the romance of being married to mujahideen (and bearing their children), of faithful sisterhood and camaraderie in an ideal state, a Muslim Utopia, appear to be irresistible.[12] Thus, notwithstanding the similarities between the rhetorical appeals made to young Western men and women to convert, in general, there is a strict gender demarcation that seems predominantly in place: the place of honor for a man is on the battlefield; for a woman, it is the home. (Virtuous) men fight and slaughter the enemy mercilessly; (good) women bear children, tend to domestic chores, and applaud their men's battlefield feats.

Nevertheless, jihadi cool/chic materials are not aimed only at potential recruits or converts. They are also aimed at third parties or bystanders: to instill awe and further spread terror, to further propagate their trademarked brutality porn, and even simply to assign to them the necessary roles of serving as spectators to their mythical feats of bravery and strength. Luke Howie astutely observed: "[C]ontemporary terrorists want a lot of people watching, not *just* a lot of people dead."[13]

A consequent question with which this book wrestles is: How does one ethically bear witness to the onslaught of such terror- and trauma-laden images and narratives (even if under the appearance of glory and heroism, as propagated by jihadi cool materials), as a third party, and not be a direct participant in their production and consumption? This book argues that there is a difference between passively consuming, as a spectator would, and critically witnessing, even if one vicariously experiences a traumatic event or experiences it through a virtual and mediated encounter, as on the internet. A witness, as Richard Quinney noted, "is moved by conscience to observe and make the report."[14] Furthermore, as Howie notes: "Witnessing is far more than merely watching or seeing. Witnesses are never passive. Witnessing is active, performed and embodied, *even when it occurs at a distance* [emphasis added]."[15] Taking this stance implies a refusal to conflate or to elide the moral differences between victims, perpetrators, and bystanders.

The ethical dilemma one faces in relation to such narratives of trauma and terror is similar to that faced by one who watches Holocaust films.[16] In Holocaust films, similar to the material examined in this book, "[j]udgment . . . is not merely portrayed but . . . *actively performed* [italics added] by [these] films, together with their . . . constructed and/or actual viewers; it is often a function of film's constitution of a community of viewers and cinematic engagement in the social constitution of primary values, institutions, and concepts."[17] Furthermore, an added dimension to Holocaust films, as well as jihadi cool material (or those that seek to counter the allure of jihadi coolness), is the question of realism, whether construed as "true," "accurate," or "realistic."[18]

Nevertheless, there is one crucial difference between many Holocaust-related films and much of the material generated by adherents of jihadi cool/chic culture. While Holocaust-related films generally shy away from what has been called by scholars of the Holocaust as the "negative sublime" of the Holocaust, the descent into the gas chambers, jihadi cool/chic materials, especially those targeted for male recruits, glory in the spectacle of brutal torture and bloody beheadings, imbuing inhumanity with the veneer of hypermasculinity. Additionally, the material is targeted to strike fear and terror in "infidel" communities. The spectatorial dynamics, to some extent, thus resemble the shock value of B-level horror films but with the technical sophistication of blockbuster Hollywood films, thus drawing in its mesmerized and horrified audiences into the power of its narrative. Nevertheless, the ethical dilemma a witness faces in light of such material remains.

The answer to such a dilemma, in my view, is pragmatic and was initially theoretically developed in relation to exploring a critical lacuna from which to view emotionally laden and historically freighted materials that potentially invite two twin dangers: (1) absolute identification (the response of the uncritical convert) and (2) absolute rejection (the response of the indifferent cynic). Such a careful balance can be maintained by a critical openness to a dialectical tension between multiple frames or points of view and a certain amount of irreducibility. In other words, this project finds an analogue in Ariella Azoulay's analysis of the hermeneutic of the photographic moment: "With the assistance of the spectator, the point of view under consideration . . . permits the event of photography to be preserved as one bearing the potential for permanent renewal that undermines any attempt to terminate it or to proclaim that it has reached its end."[19]

Nevertheless, the crucial question remains: How does one move from a deconstructive turn, which seems simply a revolving door of warring narratives, toward what I term a poethics of producing and viewing various artifacts that have assimilated the look of the "real" while being unavoidably embedded in the politics and aesthetics of such trauma- and terror-infused narratives?[20]

By "poethics" I mean, generally, the same kind of project Richard Weisberg alludes to, after the Nietzschean "*Umwertung der Werte*"[21] (roughly translated, not simply an "overturning" of values but their "re-evaluation" or "trans-valuation"): a project that "endeavors nothing less than to fill the ethical void in which legal thought and practice . . . [in which] literature [and in this book, mediated artefacts, whether they be video, film or photography, for example] provid[e] a lively and accessible medium for learning about law [and terrorism/counter-terrorism] in an ethical way."[22]

This approach is particularly evident in prior sections in relation to critically interacting with both the popular and legal narratives in relation to *Raza v. New York*. The jurisprudence that resulted from *Raza* sharply outlined the differences between an Equal Protection claim based on the Fourteenth Amendment and a Fourth Amendment search and seizure claim. At the discovery stage, as the court carefully reasoned, an Equal Protection claim is not defeated purely by a claim of reasonable suspicion or probable cause for surveillance or investigations because an element of an Equal Protection claim is proving the defendant's discriminatory animus. Combined with the broad construction of discovery principles, the Equal Protection Clause thus imposes limits on impermissible class-based discriminations, such as one based on Islam, generally construed, in this case.

Applying a poethics of witnessing requires one to critically note assumptions both sides relied upon, and one assumption that both the plaintiffs and defendants based their arguments on was that Islam—broadly construed, with no distinctions between Salafism, Jihadism, or Salafi-Jihadism—was the necessary rhetorical and pragmatic battleground upon which contestations had to be waged. In so doing, through their pleadings, both sides essentially and ironically affirmed that Islam is the gateway toward the final stage of Jihadization. Numerous experts, as explained earlier, have argued that the complex analysis of the numerous factors that influence self-radicalization has revealed this conclusion to be fallacious. By agreeing on that assumption, both parties ended up endorsing the Radicalization Model while negotiating, apparently to take down the website on this model. However, there are indications that the Radicalization Model is still being used in relation to keeping surveillance on, investigating and prosecuting individuals, both on the right and the left of the political spectrum.[23] Nevertheless, by parsing out this assumption and being critical of it, one may navigate carefully past the Scylla and Charybdis or twin dangers of being an uncritical adherent of extremes or being an indifferent outsider, a different type of extreme.

As to the popular narratives regarding *Raza v. City of New York*, depending on one's politics, one side cast it as a David versus Goliath narrative where the behemoth of government power, the police, engaged in systematic and comprehensive discrimination against all Muslims in the United States and were stopped through the assiduous efforts of religious and community leaders and several nongovernmental entities. The other side cast a narrative where they admitted no wrongdoing by settling the matter. Nevertheless, again, both narratives hinged on a polar narrative of us versus them, with being Muslim being the hinge point of difference. By placing the emphasis on markers of race, religion, or ideology, both popular narratives missed the mark of staying focused on evidence-based investigations, while staying attuned to the complex interplay of these factors with a sensitive and alert eye to enforcing domestic criminal and civil law.[24]

Unlike *Raza v. New York*, which leaves room for the revolving door of competing narratives, the story of the systematic atrocities committed against the Yazidis—acts that rise to the level of genocide, war crimes, and international human rights abuses—leaves no room for debate or relativism. The dark underside of jihadi cool/chic's romantic veneer, in its savagery and inhumanity, rises to the surface, challenging the passive spectator to become an active witness. There is something about the absolute systematization of torture, enslavement, sexual enslavement, indoctrination, and other genocidal acts that cries out for an ethical engagement rather than a passive consumption of narratives.

The similarities between the Holocaust and the genocide of the Yazidis provide fertile ground for comparison, especially in terms of their systematization. In his critically acclaimed book analyzing the modern preconditions for the Holocaust exterminations, Zygmunt Bauman quoted American Holocaust scholar Henry L. Feingold on how the mass exterminations proceeded in a seemingly innocent and routinary way:

> [Auschwitz] was also a mundane extension of the modern factory system. Rather than producing goods, the raw material was human beings and the end-product was death, so many units per day marked carefully on the manager's production charts. The chimneys, the very symbol of the modern factory system, poured forth the smoke produced by burning human flesh. The brilliantly organized railroad grid of modern Europe carried a new kind of raw material to the factories. It did so in the same manner as with other cargo. In the gas chambers the victims inhaled noxious gas generated by prussic acid pellets, which were produced by the advanced chemical industry

> of Germany. Engineers designed the crematoria; managers designed the system of bureaucracy that worked with a zest and efficiency more backward nations would envy. Even the overall plan itself was a reflection of the modern scientific spirit gone awry. What we witnessed was nothing less than a massive scheme of social engineering.[25]

In the case of the Yazidi genocide, the raw materials were members of the Yazidi tribe, and the end products were their death, torture, or enslavement, with "units" carefully cataloged and recorded. The virtual and actual slave markets, where Yazidi females were forced to parade their physical assets, such as their hair or teeth, as if on a catwalk, were a "natural" offshoot of today's fashion-oriented, social media–driven global culture. Its managers designed a system of bureaucracy, backed by a certain "scholarly" and "scriptural" justification, which reduced the Yazidis into interchangeable and dispensable units of property that could be gifted, rented, used, abused, and discarded. The overall scheme itself seemed a direct offshoot of jihadi cool/chic culture, brought to its natural conclusion: the socialized, glamorized representations of "brave" jihadi warriors and their brides forged through the enslavement, torture, humiliation, and death of all Yazidis.

Bauman also specifically coined the complex notion of *adiaphorization* to account for the voiding of action of moral content in modern society, and instead making the evaluation of actions (or inactions) based on, for instance, efficiency, technical precision, and in the case of jihadi cool/chic, a certain kind of glamour (as opposed to beauty).[26] For Bauman, adiaphorization, in an ironic reversal of the cinematic montage effect, which fills in gaps to build a coherent narrative, refers to the fragmentation of sequences of action into small, distinct units, thus blurring the causal chain of ramifications flowing from one action to another, ultimately creating a vacuum that vindicates the acting individual for his or her actions or failures to act.

In addition, adiaphorization also condenses the victim or target into a stereotype of seemingly easily recognizable attributes or derogatorily constructed qualities (e.g., the "Jew" or "Yazidi"; the "kuffar" or "infidel") thus effacing the very humanity of the victim. The natural offshoots of adiaphorization processes are moral indifference and dehumanization. Adiaphorization is thus the term that can be used to capture:

> the stripping of human relationships of their moral significance, exempting them from moral evaluation, rendering them "morally irrelevant". Adiaphorization is set in motion whenever the relationship involves less than the total person, whenever the object of the relationship is a selected aspect . . . since it is only the *full* relationship, a relationship between spatially and temporally *whole* selves, that may be "moral", that is embrace the issue of responsibility for the other. Preventing the looking from turning into seeing is . . . a major mechanism of adiaphorization.[27]

Clearly, mechanisms of adiaphorization were at work in setting up the spectacles of the genocide, mass enslavement, and sexual enslavement of the Yazidis. With the reduction of Yazidi identities to being merely "dirty kuffar" or chattel, the warrior-owners' (and their families') actions in relation to their "property" became stripped of any moral significance. This occurred save in ironic reversals, such as in the beliefs that taking slaves was an act of religious significance, and that raping an "infidel" was a "spiritual" experience.

Ultimately, breaking away from the myth of jihadi cool/chic entails a return to a perspective stressing a personal and unconditional moral responsibility for the Other—no matter who or where the other is—as the most effective, and perhaps the sole, fortification against adiaphorization and the accompanying "moral blindness" that has come to define our heavily mediated society.[28] Bauman's moral sociology owes much to the phenomenological philosophy of Emmanuel Lévinas, whose fulcrum is the unconditional responsibility for the Other, which is actualized by the encounter of seeing the face of the other—a Face capturing the innate humanity and vulnerability of other human beings through whom the presence of an infinite Other shines forth. This Face of the Other challenges and requires the actor to participate and to help.[29] *Being-for-the-Other* thus precedes merely *being-with-the-other*, which means one's moral *responsibility* in relation to an Infinite Other, glimpsed through the face of an other, takes precedence over other commitments, duties, or obligations. This unconditional responsibility of Lévinas and Bauman cannot be discarded, distributed, pawned, consigned, divested, or transferred unto others.[30] Because it is *my* responsibility and *mine* alone (and because I am ultimately always guilty before a divine Other), it inexorably remains my burden, but without this thorough-going responsibility, rationalizations, repudiations, abdications, and shrewd techniques of passivation will be resorted to in order to escape it. Like Lévinas, Bauman's understanding of moral responsibility ultimately hinges on an immediate proximity to the other (enabling a face-to-face encounter, through whom the Face of the Other may be glimpsed), and he admits that such a Levinasian morality of proximity faces[31] clear hurdles in a world increasingly mediatized between the realms of the real and the reel.

Along a parallel track, Orit Kamir created an analytically useful framework that may be deployed in differentiating between the master narrative jihadi cool/chic espouses and an alternative narrative of human dignity and respect, to which one must ultimately return, if one were to actively counter jihadi cool/chic culture.[32] She distinguished between human dignity, glory, respect, and honor as values that characterize different communities, both virtual and real. She defined human dignity as "the inherent [or innate] value of the enlightenment-based worldview ascribes to anyone who belongs to the human family."[33] She stated:

> Dignity is an ethical *ought* and not an empirical *is*; it is normative and not descriptive, quality and not quantity. Human dignity does not depict people's empirical value; it constitutes them as normatively worthy by virtue of their humanity.[34]

Drawing from Kantian philosophy,[35] and drawing a similarity to Lévinas's and Bauman's infinite responsibility to the Other/other, human dignity is the moral value of human subjects qua human subjects; as such, it must always be recognized, protected, and maintained unequivocally. Thus, it is an imperative that one must not waive the recognition of human dignity, thus treating a human being as purely an object, or a means to an end rather than an end in itself. The United Nations General Assembly's adoption of the Universal Declaration of Human Rights (UDHR) on December 10, 1948, clearly emphasized the value of dignity. In its opening sentence, the declaration stated that "recognition of the inherent dignity and of the equal and inalienable rights of all members of the human family is the foundation of freedom, justice and peace in the world."[36] As Kamir pointed out:

> This clarification came in the aftermath of World War II and the unprecedented brutality that members of the human family forced on

> each other. Horrified by humankind's unleashed potential for cruel self-destruction, the world realized and declared that future human survival and prosperity ("freedom, justice and peace in the world")[37] depended upon a universal acceptance of the tenet of human dignity.[38]

Kamir deployed the term "glory" to refer to "the value that Judeo-Christian theologies attribute to humans as manifesting God's exceptional virtue."[39] In the Judeo-Christian tradition,[40] since Adam was made in God's image and likeness, "[g]lory was thus Adam's innate, eternal, inestimable value as God's earthly image."[41] Kamir clarified the distinction between "dignity" and "glory" historically.

> Although this type of human value was traditionally called "glory," since 1948, many refer to it as "dignity." I believe that the notion of glory was the Judeo-Christian transcendental precursor of the U[niversal] D[eclaration of] H[uman] R[ight]'s humanistic, secular, enlightenment-based notion of human dignity. I suggest that the clear terminological and conceptual distinction between them is now inseparable from our civilization's separation of state from church/religion; of secular ethical values from theological ones; and of civic codes of norms from religious ones.[42]

In contrast, while valuing human dignity affirms our common humanity, respect celebrates difference. For Kamir, while human dignity is the "family (normative) attribute we all share," personal identity is "built over time; it is fluid and ever changing."[43] Thus, the term "'human dignity' assigns worth strictly to the generic stamp of fundamental humanity in each of us; to our common human denominator."[44] In comparison, respect "implies accepting recognition of multiple, concrete, unique individual identities."[45] While human dignity imbues absolute, unconditional merit and protection to a singular, generic human structure, respect, which is complementary, provides relative, tentative, and conditional value to "countless actual manifestations of human plurality."[46] Although respect-based rights are more tenuous than human dignity-based rights, they better fit a greater variety of "human needs, preferences, choices and aspirations."[47]

In stark contrast to human dignity and respect-based cultures are cultures based on honor and shame. Honor is the "relative value attributed to and felt by a member of society vis-a-vis his peers."[48] Unlike human dignity-based rights, which posit an innate and universal human structure or nature, honor and shame societies value "comparative social status, prestige, rank, and standing in the hierarchical structure of a specific group."[49] Shame is the converse of honor—its inherent lack or circumstantial loss. Honor may be partially bequeathed or inherited, but it is usually gained through consistent and strict adherence to the norms outlined by a society's honor code. The loss of honor, through a failure to abide by the dictates of the honor code, results in shame and harsh consequences. In honor and shame societies, "[h]onor is ceaselessly achieved, enhanced, accrued, and inevitably lost, while shame is dreaded and avoided at all costs."[50] Thus, in an honor-revering culture, peers are in constant competition for honor, which is hierarchical, such that one member's promotion necessarily entails the demotion of another. For Kamir, although anthropologists have described principally traditional militant cultures as honor and shame societies, the honor mentality is very much alive in contemporary cultures, which often fluctuate, to varying degrees, between a universalistic, humanistic, and dignity-based foundational attitude and a competition-based, relative, zero-sum value system.[51]

Thus, the application of this framework unveils how much virtual societies adhere to honor and shame value systems.[52] "Honor," (i.e., status and self-worth) within social media communities is based on "other members quantified, ritualized, virtual responses (such as 'likes,' 'shares,' 'follows,' and 'retweets')," mobilized by the "popularity principle that serves the commercial interests of conglomerates, and enforces the logic of zero-sum competition for precedence."[53] "Virtual shaming" determines the constantly fluctuating hierarchy, and the persistent anxiety of losing status—FOMO (fear of missing out)—is ubiquitous.

Thus, the application to the culture and narratives of jihadi cool/chic emerges spontaneously. In the virtual worlds of the internet and social media, glamorous and mythicized narratives recast traditional Muslim narratives of jihad or holy war, of martyrdom, and of "an ideal, universal Muslim nation, neo-*umma*."[54](In Islam, "Ummah" (Arabic: أُمَّة) refers to the global community of Muslims, united by their shared faith and belief in the oneness of God (Allah) and the prophethood of Muhammad.) In these virtual platforms, jihad and martyrdom are conjoined to cement suicidal warfare against what is constructed as the West's humiliation of Islam and of Muslims. Individuals who see themselves as being denied the opportunity to achieve their full potential embrace this narrative and are convinced that by committing suicidal terrorist attacks, they honor the neo-*umma* and redeem their honor as Muslims, attempting to gain honor, mistaking it for self-worth. The movements from the realm of the "reel" to the reality of the "real" and vice versa lead to a vicious cycle.

> Virtual versions of jihad, martyrdom and neo-*umma*, therefore, turn into real-world fundamentalism, and promote real-world populist nationalism that uses social media to reject opposition and criticism. Virtual jihad and martyrdom, real-world fundamentalism, and real-world populist nationalism shielded by social media all manifest escape from dignity and respect to honor.[55]

Following Kamir's lead, a return to the cultures/narratives of human dignity and respect as part of the "cure" to counter jihadi cool/chic is necessary. Another part of the "cure" would be a critical revaluation of the often unthinking adoption of the norms underlying platforms encouraging virtual connectedness, which have underlying corporate commercial interests in increasing their users' connectivity recast as "popularity." The pervasiveness of the enterprise is reflected in the successful redefinition of everyday words such as "share," "friend," and "like." As José van Dijck observed:

> In less than eight years, the meaning of "sharing," once understood as user-to-user information exchange, has been subtly replaced by a meaning that naturalizes the sharing of personal data with anyone on the planet. Among teenagers, the idea of "friending" as building the largest possible network of contacts—a social badge of honor informed by the popularity principle—has been steadily on the rise. The concept of "liking" pushes popular ideas or things with a high degree of emotional value, arguably at the expense of rational judgments for which there are no buttons in the online universe, "difficult but important" is not a judgment prompted by social media sites. Sharing, friending and liking are powerful ideological concepts whose impact reaches beyond Facebook proper into all corners of culture, affecting the very fabric of sociality.[56]

The mechanisms of the virtual honor game promote zero-sum competition, hierarchical thinking (at the apex of which are "influencers"), the maintenance of group norms (encoded by commercial platforms), the formation of strategic alliances, the exposure of competitors, and shaming, among other features, at the expense of privacy, authenticity, and empathy, which characterize communities of human dignity, glory, and respect. Perhaps hardly surprisingly, the transparent algorithm-fabricated honor norms that further commercial platforms' profit interests have a spontaneous affinity with jihadi cool/chic's norms because they promote the treatment of human beings as things, instead of as ends in themselves. The real-life abuse and genocide of the Yazidi people are a natural outflow of this real/reel honor society because shaming, whose extreme example is the justified abuse, rape, and mass murder of the "dirty kuffar," are an integral part of its mechanisms. It is through the "infidel's" degradation that one gains honor (and apparent glory as "in most cases, religion is no more than a pretext"[57]) individually, collectively, and in the name of Islam. Another way one gains honor, within the virtual and real universe of jihadi cool/chic, is by sacrificing oneself in a transnational Muslim holy war through jihadist martyrdom. It is with a violent death that maximizes harm to the "enemies" of Islam that a pathway seems to open up, through which one finally seems to attain a form of dignity and respect normally not accessible in real life. Constructing a narrative that unmasks this as a lie is also another part of the "cure" to the myths of jihadi cool/chic and engaging with jihadists.

There have been several initiatives, started by nongovernmental entities, which took ISIS's own narrative strategies and techniques as weapons against them. One such example was the generation of anti-ISIS videos on the Open Your Eyes website, which appeared to have broad currency on YouTube and other social media for a time.

The Open Your Eyes initiative began when three young Yazidi women, who had suffered extreme sexual abuse at the hands of ISIS, visited the UK, under government sponsorship, to recount their experiences to the media, politicians, and children at two schools. The Yazidis then forged an alliance with a Birmingham-based activist group, "Upstanding Neighbourhoods," to launch the Open Your Eyes campaign, with financial backing from the international charity AMAR Foundation.[58]

Like ISIS, the Open Your Eyes initiative used various forms of social media for a spectrum of purposes. Its Twitter account stated: "ISIS is lying to you. Open your eyes to the real story. We are working with young people, activists, bloggers and filmmakers to raise our voices against ISIS." One of its tweets urged that "Open Your Eyes needs your contributions—send in your video messages to take a stand against ISIS."

In a manner that mimed, but deconstructed, jihadi cool/chic videos, the various videos posted on Open Your Eyes deployed first-person narratives. In one of its videos, Krya, a young girl wearing a black headscarf, discussed British girls migrating to join ISIS. In another, Sabah, a Sunni who escaped ISIS in Iraq, recounted his experiences. A different video featured an 18-year-old schoolboy, Surfaraz, who said he chose to speak up "because [he didn't] want anyone to be brainwashed by lies."[59] Of notable interest was the use of documentary techniques of filmic narration, particularly as remedies to jihadi cool/chic's mythic simulation of both classic Hollywood cinematic narration and the verisimilitude of gaming videos.

Conclusion

Summarizing this book succinctly, Chapter 1 described the rhetorical and aesthetic dimensions of jihadi cool/chic, which appear to be crucial factors in the generation of self-radicalizing individuals. This chapter thus sought to recreate, with precision, the aestheticization of violence that the phenomenon of the jihadi cool/chic amounted to as a virtual campaign tailored to the dominant codes of social networks in liberal societies. This chapter clarified the construction of gender roles and the humanization of jihadis through an analysis of narrative modes of visual performance that are rooted in the visual culture of social media.

Chapter 2 analyzed the jurisprudence and larger legal and cultural ramifications that sprang from *Raza v. New York*. The *Raza* ruling effectively pulled the New York Police Department back from the practice of treating all Islamic institutions as breeding grounds for radicalization—a discriminatory practice that violated their religious rights. This chapter genealogized, great technical detail, the relevant case law that enabled the *Raza* court to parse out distinctions between Fourth Amendment and Equal Protection litigation in granting broad discovery to plaintiffs seeking to establish discrimination claims. Crucial to the setting of the stage for the in-depth discussion of *Raza* was the explication of the historical background that preceded this litigation, especially in connection with the collaboration between intelligence agencies and the NYPD. Of equal import was the critical review of theories of radicalization and their assumptions because these underlie the government policies and procedures that seek to counter the process of self-radicalization.

Chapter 3 engaged in an in-depth analysis—as a deconstructive legal and cultural counter-narrative—of the Yazidi genocide as the natural real-world offshoot of jihadi cool/chic. The most overtly legal in construction and probative force, this chapter offered an extremely detailed account of the genocide perpetrated by ISIS on the Yazidi people. It also analyzed the ideological grounds that motivated and justified such a gruesome and systematic destruction, reminiscent of the Holocaust.

Chapter 4 was the most overtly philosophical of the chapters, and was the Ariadnean thread that undergirded and drove the continuity across the chapters. It laid out a theory of witnessing that draws from Levinasian and Kantian ethics to engage the responsibility of the reader in bearing witness to the subject matter the book analyzed. Rather than attempting to create an ultimate master narrative to counteract jihadi cool/chic, this chapter instead analyzed the hidden assumptions that underlay the legal and cultural dynamics in *Raza v. New York* to illustrate that both sides ironically assumed one of jihadi cool/chic's corollaries: that Islam is the gateway to radicalization. It outlined the virtual and real foundations of honor and shame that underlie jihadi cool/chic culture (and social media networks in general) and explored the conditions of possibility within which a return to narratives/cultures of human dignity, glory, and respect could be preliminarily reconstructed and a critical engagement with jihadists could be initiated. This chapter concentrated the insights that animated this research project in its genesis and development.

As a final note, this book closes with a caveat from Friedrich Nietzsche that resonates with some of the concluding insights of this book: "He who fights with monsters might take care lest he thereby becomes a monster. And when you gaze long into an abyss the abyss also gazes into you."[60]

Notes

1 A preliminary analysis of the roles the internet plays in the formation of self-radicalizing individuals occurs in Caroline Joan S. Picart, "Jihad Cool/Jihad Chic: The Roles of the Internet and Imagined Relations in the Self-Radicalization of Colleen LaRose (Jihad Jane)," *Societies* 5 (April 2015): 354–83; doi: 10.3390/soc5020354.

2 Sageman's four stages are: (1) moral outrage about the suffering of fellow Muslims, (2) the fit between this outrage and an individual's worldview, (3) the resonance of the jihadist interpretation with an individual's personal everyday experiences, and (4) mobilization by already existing networks. Marc Sageman, *Leaderless Jihad: Terror Networks in the Twenty-First Century* (Philadelphia: University of Pennsylvania Press, 2008), 71–88.

3 Ibid. at 72.

4 "Violent Extremism: How Are People Moved from Constitutionally-Protected Thought to Acts of Terrorism?," Hearing Before S. Comm. on Intelligence, Information Sharing and Terror Risk Assessment of the Hearing Before the H. Comm. on Homeland Sec., 111th Congress, 3 (2009) (testimony of Kim Cragin, RAND Corporation). See also: Kim Cragin, "Understanding Terrorist Ideology, Testimony presented before the S. Select Comm. on Intelligence," *RAND Corporation*, June 12, 2007, http://www.rand.org/pubs/testimonies/CT338.html.

5 Ibid.; Brian Michael Jenkins, "Would-be Warriors: Incidents of Jihadist Terrorist Radicalization in the United States Since September 11, 2001," *RAND Corporation*, May 5, 2010, at 7, http://www.rand.org/pubs/occasional_papers/OP292.html.

6 Clark McCauley and Sophia Moskalenko, "Individual and Group Mechanisms of Radicalization," in *Topical Strategic Multi-Layer Assessment (SMA), Multi-Agency and Air Force Research Laboratory, Multi-Disciplinary White Papers in Support of Counter-Terrorism and Counter-WMD*, ed. Laurie Fenstermacher, 2010, at 82, 88, accessed September 5, 2016 http://www.start.umd.edu/sites/default/files/files/publications/U_Counter_Terrorism_White_Paper_Final_January_2010.pdf.

7 Sharon Behn, "ISIS Militants Use 'Jihadi Cool' to Recruit Globally," *VOA News*, September 5, 2014, at 34, http://www.voanews.com/content/isis-militants-use-jihadi-cool-to-recruit-globally/2440430.html.

8 Mauro, "ISIS: 'Cool' Image Winning Over Next Generation of Jihadis," *Clarion Project*, August 31, 2014, https://web.archive.org/web/20150720192107/http:/www.clarionproject.org/analysis/islamic-state-winning-over-next-generation-jihadis.

9 Behn, "ISIS Militants Use 'Jihadi Cool' to Recruit Globally."

10 Gabriel Weimann, "New Terrorism and New Media," *Wilson Center*, 2014, https://www.wilsoncenter.org/sites/default/files/media/documents/publication/STIP_140501_new_terrorism_F.pdf.

11 *See, e.g.*, Barbara Plett Usher, "The US Department's YouTube 'Digital Jihad'," BBC, November 28, 2014, http://www.bbc.com/news/magazine-30045038; Avidan Milevsky, "Why are Teens Joining ISIS?," *Huffington Post*, September 8, 2014, 3:57, accessed November 8, 2014, http://www.huffingtonpost.com/avidan-milevsky/why-are-teens-joining-isi_b_5773668.html.

12 *See, e.g.*, Beenish Ahmed, "How A Teenage Girl Goes From Listening To Coldplay And Reading Harry Potter To Joining ISIS," *ThinkProgress*, February 24, 2015, accessed September 6, 2016, https://archive.thinkprogress.org/how-a-teenage-girl-goes-from-listening-to-coldplay-and-reading-harry-potter-to-joining-isis-1fc8f64526d5/; Carolyn Hoyle, Alexandra Bradford, and Ross Frenett, "Becoming Mulan? Female Western Migrants to ISIS," *Institute for Strategic Dialogue*, 2015, accessed September 6, 2016, https://www.isdglobal.org/wp-content/uploads/2016/02/ISDJ2969_Becoming_Mulan_01.15_WEB.pdf.

13 Luke Howie, *Witnesses to Terror: Understanding the Meanings and Consequences of Terrorism* (London: Palgrave Macmillan, 2012), at 160.

14 Richard Quinney, "Who Is The Victim?," *Criminology* 10, no. 2 (November 1972): 207.

15 Howie, *Witnesses to Terror*, at 20.

16 *See, e.g.*, David Shneer, *Through Soviet Jewish Eyes: Photography, War, and the Holocaust* (New Brunswick: Rutgers University Press, 2012), at 140–83; and Caroline Joan "Kay" S. Picart and David A. Frank, *Frames of Evil: The Holocaust as Horror in American Film* (Carbondale: Southern Illinois University Press, 2006), at 126–46.

17 Orit Kamir, "Cinematic Judgment and Jurisprudence: A Woman's Memory, Recovery and Justice in a Post-Traumatic Society (A Study of Polanski's Death

and the Maiden)," in *Law on the Screen*, ed. Austin Sarat, Lawrence Douglas, and Martha Merrill Umphrey (Princeton: Princeton University Press, 2005), at 28–9.

18 For an account that analyzes *The Godfather Trilogy* as Francis Ford Coppola's attempt to demythologize America as "a pluralistic society living by the rule of law and serving as a model for the rest of the world," see David Ray Papke, "Myth and Meaning: Francis Ford Coppola and Popular Response to the Godfather Trilogy," in *Legal Reelism: Movies as Legal Texts*, ed. John Denvir (Champaign: University of Illinois Press, 1996), at 1–22

19 Ariella Azoulay, *Photography*, Mafte'akh 2e, 79 (2011), accessed June 1, 2024, http://mafteakh.tau.ac.il/en/wp-content/uploads/2011/01/Photography.pdf.

20 Some of these ideas were first proposed in Caroline Joan "Kay" S. Picart, "Nationalities, Histories, Rhetorics: Real/Reel Representations of the Holocaust and Holocaust Trials and a Poethics of Film and Law," *Dapim: Studies on the Holocaust* 29, no. 2 (May 2015): 17–19, copyright© Institute for Holocaust Research, University of Haifa, reprinted by permission of Taylor & Francis Ltd, http://www.tandfonline.com on behalf of Institute for Holocaust Research, University of Haifa. The author thanks the staff of *Dapim* and Taylor and Francis.

21 Richard Weisberg, *Poethics and Other Strategies of Law and Literature* (New York: Columbia University Press, 1992), at xii.

22 Ibid. at 4–5.

23 For an attempt to nuance the Radicalization Model into a Radicalization Trajectory, *see* Jytte Klausen, "A Behavioral Study of the Radicalization Trajectories of American 'Homegrown' Al Qaeda-Inspired Terrorist Offenders," *U.S. Department of Justice*, November 2016, https://www.ojp.gov/pdffiles1/nij/grants/250417.pdf.

24 *See also* Mike German, "20th Anniversary of 9/11 Special Edition Lessons for the Next Twenty Years: What We've Learned in the Two Decades Since 9/11; a Project of Syracuse University's Institute for Security Policy and Law: Part IV—Domestic Terror and the Fight to Sustain Democracy: Learning from Our Mistakes: How Not to Confront White Supremacist Violence," *Journal of National Security Law and Policy* 12, no. 1 (2021): 169, 169–77.

25 Feingold quoted in Zygmunt Bauman, *Modernity and the Holocaust* (Cambridge: Polity Press, 1989), 8.

26 For a detailed exposition of Zygmunt Bauman's moral sociology, as applied to the Holocaust and postmodernity, see Michael Hviid Jacobsen, "Evil-by-Proxy and Everyday Monsters: Toward a Moral Sociology for Overcoming the

Passive Observation of Evil," in *Monsters, Law, Crime: Explorations in Gothic Criminology*, ed. Caroline Joan "Kay" S. Picart (Lanham: Fairleigh Dickinson University Press, 2021), 97–119.

27 Zygmunt Bauman, *Life in Fragments: Essays in Postmodern Reality* (Oxford: Blackwell Publishers, 1995), 133–4.

28 Zygmunt Bauman and Leonidas Donskis, *Moral Blindness—The Loss of Sensitivity in Liquid Modernity* (Cambridge: Polity Press, 2013).

29 Roger Burggraeve, "Violence and the Vulnerable Face of the Other: The Vision of Emmanuel Levinas on Moral Evil and Our Responsibility," *Journal of Social Philosophy* 30, no. 1 (1999): 29–45.

30 Zygmunt Bauman, *Postmodern Ethics* (Oxford: Blackwell, 1993), 250.

31 Zygmunt Bauman, "The World Inhospitable to Levinas," *Philosophy Today* 43, no. 2 (1999): 151–67.

32 Orit Kamir, *Betraying Dignity: The Toxic Seduction of Social Media, Shaming, and Radicalization* (Lanham: Fairleigh Dickinson University Press, 2020).

33 Ibid. at xvii.

34 Ibid., emphasis in original.

35 See generally, Immanuel Kant, *Groundwork of the Metaphysics of Morals* (1784), trans. Thomas Kingsmill Abbott (Peterborough: Broadview, 2005).

36 UN General Assembly, UDHR, Article 1; Preamble.

37 Ibid.

38 Kamir, *Betraying Dignity*, xviii.

39 Ibid.

40 Kamir limits her analysis to the Judeo-Christian tradition.

41 Kamir, *Betraying Dignity*, xviii.

42 Ibid. at xix.

43 Ibid.

44 Ibid.

45 Ibid. at xx.

46 Ibid.

47 Ibid.

48 Ibid.

49 Ibid.

50 Ibid. at xxi.

51 Ibid.

52 Kamir sees a more wide-ranging application to the framework, including victimhood culture, among others. I limit the use of the framework to an analysis of the dynamics of jihadi cool/chic and self-radicalization.

53 Kamir, *Betraying Dignity*, 140.

54 Ibid.

55 Ibid. at 141.

56 José van Dijck, *The Culture of Connectivity: A Critical History of Social Media* (New York: Oxford University Press, 2013), 65–6.

57 Farhad Khosrokhavar, *Suicide Bombers: Allah's New Martyrs*, translated by David Mace (London: Pluto, 2005), 47.

58 Susannah Tarbush, "New British Initiatives Aim to Counter ISIS on Social Media," *The Tanjara*, August 28, 2015.

59 Formerly available at: http://openyoureyes.net/.

60 Friedrich Nietzsche, *Jenseits von Gut und Böse. Zur Genealogie der Moral (1886)*, ed. Giorgio Colli and Mazzino Montinari (Munich, Germany: dtv Verlagsgesellschaft mbH & Co KG, 1999, reprint 2002), Aphorism 146.

Bibliography

Ahmed, Beenish. "How A Teenage Girl Goes from Listening to Coldplay and Reading Harry Potter to Joining ISIS." *ThinkProgress*, February 24, 2015. https://archive.thinkprogress.org/how-a-teenage-girl-goes-from-listening-to-coldplay-and-reading-harry-potter-to-joining-isis-1fc8f64526d5/.

Akbar, Amna. "National Security's Broken Windows." *UCLA Law Review* 62 (2015): 834–907.

Alami, Mona. "Al-Qaeda Using Magazines to Spread Message." *USA Today*, April 20, 2011. http://usatoday30.usatoday.com/news/world/2011-04-19-al-qaeda-magazines.htm.

Al-Tamimi, Aymenn Jawad. "Archive of Islamic State Administrative Documents (cont.)." *Pundicity Informed Opinion & Review*, January 11, 2016. http://www.aymennjawad.org/2016/01/archive-of-islamic-state-administrative-documents-1.

Al-Tamini, Aymenn Jawad. "Unseen Islamic State Pamphlet on Slavery (translated by Aymenn Jawad Al-Tamimi)." *Pundicity Informed Opinion & Review*, December 29, 2015. http://www.aymennjawad.org/2015/12/unseen-islamic-state-pamphlet-on-slavery.

Aptel, Cécile. "Child Slaves and Child Brides." *Journal of International Criminal Justice* 14, no. 2 (2016): 1–21.

Apuzzo, Matt and Adam Goldman. *Enemies Within: Inside the NYPD's Secret Spying Unit and Bin Laden's Final Plot Against America*. New York: Simon & Schuster, 2013.

Apuzzo, Matt and Adam Goldman. "With CIA Help, NYPD Moves Covertly in Muslim Areas." *The Pulitzer Prizes: The 2012 Pulitzer Prize Winner in Investigative Reporting*, August 24, 2011. https://www.pulitzer.org/winners/matt-apuzzo-adam-goldman-eileen-sullivan-and-chris-hawley.

Ashcroft v. Iqbal, 556 U.S. 662, 677, 129 S. Ct. 1937, 173 L. Ed. 2D 868 (2009).

Askin, Kelly. "Women's Issues in International Criminal Law: Recent Developments and the Potential Contribution of the ICC." In *International Crimes, Peace and Human Rights: the Role of the International Criminal Court*, edited by Dinah Shelton, 47–52. Netherlands: Martinus Nijhoff, 2000.

Azoulay, Ariella. "Photography." *Mafte'akh* 2e 79 (2011). http://mafteakh.tau.ac.il/en/wp-content/uploads/2011/01/Photography.pdf.

Barnard, Anne and Alan Feuer. "Outraged, and Outrageous." *The New York Times*, October 8, 2010. http://www.nytimes.com/2010/10/10/nyregion/10geller.html.

Bauman, Zygmunt. *Life in Fragments: Essays in Postmodern Reality*. Oxford: Blackwell Publishers, 1995.

Bauman, Zygmunt. *Modernity and the Holocaust*. Cambridge: Polity Press, 1989.

Bauman, Zygmunt. *Postmodern Ethics*. Oxford: Blackwell, 1993.

Bauman, Zygmunt. "The World Inhospitable to Levinas." *Philosophy Today* 43, no. 2 (1999): 151–67.

Bauman, Zygmunt and Leonidas Donskis. *Moral Blindness-The Loss of Sensitivity in Liquid Modernity*. Cambridge: Polity Press, 2013.

Behn, Sharon. "ISIS Militants Use 'Jihadi Cool' to Recruit Globally." *VOA News*, September 5, 2014. http://www.voanews.com/content/isis-militants-use-jihadi-cool-to-recruit-globally/2440430.html.

Bosnia and Herzegovina v. Serbia and Montenegro, Application of the Convention on the Prevention and Punishment of the Crime of Genocide, ICJ Judgment, 26 February 2006, para. 344.

British Broadcasting Corporation. "Zoroastrianism at a Glance." *Zoroastrianism*, October 2, 2009. https://www.bbc.co.uk/religion/religions/zoroastrian/ataglance/glance.shtm.

Brittany, Morgan. "'Jihad Cool'—Recruiting Terrorists from America." *World Net Daily*, August 26, 2014. http://www.wnd.com/2014/08/jihad-cool-recruiting-terrorists-from-america/.

Brown v. City of Oneonta, 221 F. 3d 329, 337 (2d Cir. 1999).

Burggraeve, Roger. "Violence and the Vulnerable Face of the Other: The Vision of Emmanuel Levinas on Moral Evil and Our Responsibility." *Journal of Social Philosophy* 30, no. 1 (1999): 29–45.

Calderone, Michael. "AP's Matt Apuzzo and Adam Goldman Crack Open Secretive Institutions, from NYPD to CIA." *Huffington Post*, September 3, 2013. https://www.huffpost.com/entry/ap-nypd-matt-apuzzo-adam-goldman_n_3861444.

Chambers v. TRM Copy Centers Corp., 43 F.3d 29, 37 (2d Cir. 1994).

Complaint, *Raza v. City of New York*, No. 13-cv-3448-PKC-JMA, 5-9 (E.D.N.Y. June 18, 2013). https://www.aclu.org/national-security/raza-v-city-new-york-complaint.

"Convention on the Prevention and Punishment of the Crime of Genocide." *United Nations*. https://www.un.org/en/genocideprevention/documents/atrocity-crimes/Doc.1_Convention%20on%20the%20Prevention%20and%20Punishment%20of%20the%20Crime%20of%20Genocide.pdf.

Cottee, Simon. "Op-Ed: Islamic State's Badass Path to Paradise." *Los Angeles Times*, September 6, 2014. http://www.latimes.com/opinion/op-ed/la-oe-0907-cottee-badass-jihadi-cool-20140907-story.html#page=1.

Coyne, Jerry. "Salman Rushdie Condemns 'Jihadi Cool.'" *Why Evolution Is True*, October 12, 2014. http://whyevolutionistrue.wordpress.com/2014/10/12/salman-rushdie-condemns-jihadi-cool/.

Cragin, Kim. "Understanding Terrorist Ideology, Testimony presented before the S. Select Comm. on Intelligence." *RAND Corporation*, June 12, 2007. http://www.rand.org/pubs/testimonies/CT338.html.

Crary, David. "AP Series About NYPD Surveillance Wins Pulitzer." *Associated Press*, April 16, 2012. https://www.ap.org/ap-in-the-news/2012/ap-series-about-nypd-surveillance-wins-pulitzer.

Crenshaw, Kimberle. "Mapping the Margins: Intersectionality, Identity, Politics and Violence against Women of Color." In *Critical Race Theory: The Key Writings that Formed the Movement*, edited by Kimberle Crenshaw, Neil Gotanda, Gary Peller and Kendall Thomas, 357–83. New York: The New York Press, 1995.

Dabiq. "The Revival of Slavery Before the Hour." *Dabiq* 4 (2014): 14–16.

Dinler v. City of New York, 607 F.3d 923, 931 (2d Cir. 2010).

Dubal, Veena. "The Demise of Community Policing? The Impact of Post-9/11 Federal Surveillance Programs on Local Law Enforcement." *Asian American Law Journal* 19, no. 1 (2012): 35–59. https://lawcat.berkeley.edu/record/1124968?ln=en&v=pdf.

Emerson, Steven. "Jihadists Magazines Recruit Young Terrorists." *Algemeiner*, April 15, 2013. http://www.algemeiner.com/2013/04/15/jihadist-magazines-recruit-young-terrorists/.

Emerson, Steven. "The New York Times: Making the World Safe for Terrorism." *The Counter Jihad Report*, May 14, 2014. https://web.archive.org/web/20140519160238/http://counterjihadreport.com:80/category/nypd/.

Fleck, Ludwik. *The Genesis and Development of a Scientific Fact*. Chicago: University of Chicago Press, 1979.

German, Mike. "Learning from Our Mistakes: How Not to Confront White Supremacist Violence." *Journal of National Security Law and Policy* 12, no. 1 (June 13, 2021): 169–77.

Goldman, Adam and Matt Apuzzo. "CIA to Pull Officer from NYPD After Internal Probe." *Times West Virginian*, January 6, 2012. Accessed July 27, 2014. https://www.timeswv.com/news/national_news/cia-to-pull-officer-from-nypd-after-internal-probe/article_ce398add-de8a-5452-acff-6fc740554c7f.html.

Goldman, Adam and Matt Apuzzo. "NYPD Secretly Designated Entire Mosques as Terrorism Organizations." *Huffington Post*, August 28, 2013. http://www.huffingtonpost.com/2013/08/28/nypd-spying-mosques_n_3827567.html.

Gould, Stephen Jay. *Wonderful Life: The Burgess Shale and the Nature of History*. New York: W.W. Norton and Company, 1990.

Gray v. Board of Higher Education, City of New York, 692 F.2d 901, 906 (2d Cir. 1982).

Gurski, Phil. *The Threat from Within: Recognizing Al Qaeda-Inspired Radicalization and Terrorism in the West*. Lanham: Rowman & Littelfield Publishers, 2016.

Hagstrom, Anders. "Who is Hadi Matar? Everything We Know About Salman Rushdie's Alleged Attacker." *FOXNews*, August 15, 2022. https://www.foxnews.com/us/hadi-matar-everything-we-know-salman-rushdies-alleged-attacker.

Halverson, Jeffry R., H.L. Goodall, Jr., and Steven R. Corman. *Master Narratives of Islamist Extremism*. London: Palgrave Macmillan, 2011.

Hamid, Shadi and Rashid Dar. "Islamism, Salafism, and Jihadism: A Primer." *The Brookings Institution*, July 15, 2016. https://www.brookings.edu/blog/markaz/2016/07/15/islamism-salafism-and-jihadism-a-primer/.

Handschu v. Police Department of N.Y., 219 F. Supp. 388 (S.D.N.Y. 2016).

Handschu v. Police Department, 241 F. Supp. 3d 433, 438 (S.D.N.Y. 2017).

Handschu v. Police Department of N.Y., 905 F. Supp. 2d 555 (S.D.N.Y. 2012).

Handschu v. Special Servs. Div., 273 F. Supp. 273 F. Supp. 2d. 345 (S.D.N.Y. 2003).

Handschu v. Special Services Division, 605 F. Supp. 1384 (S.D.N.Y. 1985).

Handschu v. Special Services Division, 2007 U.S. Dist. LEXIS 43176 at 67 (S.D.N.Y. 2007).

Hawley, Chris. "Law May Not be on Muslims' Side in NYPD Intel Case." *Associated Press, San Diego* Tribune, November 7, 2011. https://www.sandiegouniontribune.com/sdut-law-may-not-be-on-muslims-side-in-nypd-intel-case-2011nov07-story.html.

Hayden v. County Of Nassau, 180 F.3d 42, 48 (2d 1999).

Heyes, J.D. "Pentagon Researching 'Narrative Networks' as Way to Hijack the Brain with False Stories." *Natural News*, May 15, 2012. https://www.naturalnews.com/035872_Pentagon_narrative_networks_propaganda.html.

Hicks, Josh. "Rep. McCaul Questions U.S. Response to 'Jihadi Cool' Threat." *Washington Post*, September 12, 2014. http://www.washingtonpost.com/blogs/federal-eye/wp/2014/09/12/rep-mccaul-questions-u-s-response-to-jihadi-cool-threat/.

Howard v. Senkowski, 986 F.2d 24, 29–30 (2d Cir, 1993).

Howie, Luke. *Witnesses to Terror: Understanding the Meanings and Consequences of Terrorism*. London: Palgrave Macmillan, 2012.

Hoyle, Carolyn, Alexandra Bradford, and Ross Frenett, "Becoming Mulan? Female Western Migrants to ISIS." *Institute for Strategic Dialogue*, 2015. https://www.isdglobal.org/wp-content/uploads/2016/02/ISDJ2969_Becoming_Mulan_01.15_WEB.pdf.

Hsu, Spencer S. "Arrest of Va. Man Spotlights Al-Qaeda's New American Recruiters." *Washington Post*, August 1, 2010. https://www.washingtonpost.com/wp-dyn/content/article/2010/07/31/AR2010073102680.html?sid=ST2010072106133.

Hunter v. Underwood, 471 U.S. 222, 225, 105 S. Ct. 1916, 85 L. Ed. 2D 222 (1985).

Hunter, Melanie. "Former Counterterror Official: 'We Don't Have Enough Muslim FBI Agents.'" *CNS News*, October 27, 2014. http://www.cnsnews.com/news/article/melanie-hunter/former-counterterror-official-we-dont-have-enough-muslim-fbi-agents.

Huq, Aziz Z. "Modeling Terrorist Radicalization." *Duke Forum for Law and Social Change* 2 (2010): 39–69. http://dflsc.law.duke.edu/article/modeling-terrorist-radicalization/.

In re Subpoena Issued to Dennis Friedman, 350 F.3d 65, 69 (2d Cir. 2003).

Intelligence Bureau, N.J. Office of Homeland Sec. & Preparedness. "Homegrown Plots: New York 2009 and Fort Dix." *Office of Homeland Security & Preparedness*, 2009. https://info.publicintelligence.net/Homegrown%20Plots-New%20York%202009%20and%20Fort%20Dix.pdf.

IPT News. "Jihad is Cool: Jihadist Magazines Recruit Young Terrorists." *Investigative Project on Terrorism*, April 11, 2013. http://www.investigativeproject.org/3969/jihad-is-cool-jihadist-magazines-recruit-young.

"Iranian Foundation Offers Land to Salman Rushdie's Attacker – State TV." *Reuters*, February 21, 2023. https://www.reuters.com/world/middle-east/iranian-foundation-offers-land-salman-rushdies-attacker-state-media-2023-02-21/.

"Iranian Foundation Praises Rushdie's Alleged Attacker, Offers Gift of Farmland." *RFE/RL's Radio Farda*, February 21, 2023. https://www.rferl.org/a/iran-rushdie-attacker-land-gift/32281094.html.

Jacobsen, Michael Hviid. "Evil-by-Proxy and Everyday Monsters: Toward a Moral Sociology for Overcoming the Passive Observation of Evil." In *Monsters, Law, Crime: Explorations in Gothic Criminology*, edited by Caroline Joan "Kay" S. Picart, 97–119. Lanham: Fairleigh Dickinson University Press, 2021.

Jalabi, Raya. "Who Are the Yazidis and Why is ISIS Hunting Them?" *The Guardian*, August 11, 2014. https://www.theguardian.com/world/2014/aug/07/who-yazidi-isis-iraq-religion-ethnicity-mountains.

Jenkins, Brian Michael. "Would-be Warriors: Incidents of Jihadist Terrorist Radicalization in the United States Since September 11, 2001." *Rand Corporation*,

May 5, 2010. Accessed June 1, 2024. http://www.rand.org/pubs/occasional_papers/OP292.html.

"The Jihad Shopping Network, Courtesy of ISIS." *Warrior*, June 24, 2014. Accessed June 1, 2024. http://warrior.scout.com/story/1414293-the-jihad-shopping-network-courtesy-of-isis.

"'Jihadi-Cool' Language Luring Young British Muslims to Islamic State, Salman Rushdie Says." *Times of India*, October 12, 2014. http://timesofindia.indiatimes.com/world/uk/Jihadi-cool-language-luring-young-British-Muslims-to-Islamic-State-Salman-Rushdie-says/articleshow/44791862.cms.

Johns, Sarah A. "The Long Term-Failings of Internally Displaced Person Status: A Case Study of the Ězidi People." *Notre Dame Journal of International and Comparative Law* 13, no. 2 (2023): 39–57.

Jones, Allen Benjamin. "Jihadi Cool." *Not Theology Blog*, July 24, 2013. https://nottheology.wordpress.com/2013/07/24/jihadi-cool-2/.

Jones, Sarah E. "Spy vs. Constitution: New York City Police Agree to Settlement in Muslim Surveillance Case." *Americans United*, January 8, 2016.

Kamir, Orit. *Betraying Dignity: The Toxic Seduction of Social Media, Shaming, and Radicalization*. Lanham: Fairleigh Dickinson University Press, 2020.

Kamir, Orit. "Cinematic Judgment and Jurisprudence: A Woman's Memory, Recovery and Justice in a Post-Traumatic Society (A Study of Polanski's Death and the Maiden)." In *Law on the Screen*, edited by Austin Sarat, Lawrence Douglas, and Martha Merrill Umphrey. Princeton: Princeton University Press, 2005.

Kant, Immanuel. *Groundwork of the Metaphysics of Morals,* translated by Thomas Kingsmill Abbott. Peterborough: Broadview, 2005.

Katz, Jack. *Seductions of Crime: Moral and Sensual Attractions in Doing Evil*. New York: Basic Books, 1988.

Keys-Turner, Karen D. "The Violent Islamic Radicalization Process: A Framework for Understanding." M.A. thesis, Naval Postgraduate School, Monterey, CA, December 2011.

Khosrokhavar, Farhad. *Suicide Bombers: Allah's New Martyrs,* translated by David Mace. London: Pluto, 2005.

Kielburger, Craig and Marc Kielburger. "No Easy Answers to Terrorist Recruitment." *Exeter Lakeshore Times Advance*, October 10, 2014. http://www.lakeshoreadvance.com/2014/10/09/how-do-young-canadians-end-up-among-the-jihadis.

Klausen, Jytte. "A Behavioral Study of the Radicalization Trajectories of American 'Homegrown' Al Qaeda-Inspired Terrorist Offenders." *U.S. Department of Justice* November 2016. https://www.ojp.gov/pdffiles1/nij/grants/250417.pdf.

Kredo, Adam. "Court Requires NYPD to Purge Documents on Terrorists Inside U.S." *The Washington Free Beacon*, January 18, 2016. https://freebeacon.com/national-security/court-requires-nypd-purge-docs-terrorists-inside-us/.

Kurdistanica.com. "Cult of Angels." *Kurdistanica: Kurdish Encyclopedia*, 2008. http://www.kurdistanica.com/?qde/101.

Larson, Eric V. "Strategic Narratives: Their Uses and Limitations." *Rand Corporation*, November 29, 2011. Accessed June 1, 2024. https://www.state.gov/documents/organization/180021.pdf.

Leigh, Karen and Bruce Crumley. "New Jihadi Recruitment Tool: Militants' Instagram Accounts." *Christian Science Monitor*, June 10, 2014. https://www.csmonitor.com/World/Middle-East/2014/0610/New-jihadi-recruitment-tool-militants-Instagram-accounts.

Lieberman, Joseph and Susan Collins. "Violent Islamist Extremism, The Internet, and the Homegrown Terrorist Threat, Majority and Minority Staff Report." United States Senate Committee on Homeland Security and Governmental Affairs, May 8, 2008. https://web.archive.org/web/20081030213611/http:/hsgac.senate.gov/public/_files/IslamistReport.pdf.

Maan, Ajit. *Counter Terrorism: Narrative Strategies*. Lanham: University Press of America, 2015.

Mauro, Ryan. "ISIS: 'Cool' Image Winning Over Next Generation of Jihadis." *Clarion Project*, August 31, 2014. https://web.archive.org/web/20150720192107/http:/www.clarionproject.org/analysis/islamic-state-winning-over-next-generation-jihadis.

"Mazdaism." *The Free Dictionary*, March 3, 2024. https://www.thefreedictionary.com/Mazdaism.

McCaul, Michael. "Islamic State Is Recruiting America's 'Jihadi Cool' Crowd." *The Wall Street Journal*, September 11, 2014. http://www.wsj.com/articles/michael-mccall-islamic-state-is-recruiting-americas-jihadi-cool-crowd-1410478638.

McCauley, Clark and Sophia Moskalenko. "Individual and Group Mechanisms of Radicalization." In *Topical Strategic Multi-Layer Assessment (SMA), Multi-Agency and Air Force Research Laboratory, Multi-Disciplinary White Papers in Support of Counter-Terrorism and Counter-WMD*, edited by Laurie Fenstermacher, 82–92. 2010. https://www.start.umd.edu/sites/default/files/publications/local_attachments/U_Counter_Terrorism_White_Paper_Final_January_2010.pdf.

McKinnon, Catharine A. "Rape, Genocide, and Women's Human Rights." *Harvard Women's Law Journal* 17, no. 5 (1994): 5–16.

Metropolitan Life Insurance Company v. RJR Nabisco, Inc., 906 F.2d 884, 891 (2d Cir. 1990).

Milevsky, Avidan. "Why are Teens Joining ISIS?" *The Huffington Post*, September 8, 2014. http://www.huffingtonpost.com/avidan-milevsky/why-are-teens-joining-isi_b_5773668.html.

"Mithraism." *Encyclopedia Britannica*, March 3, 2024. https://www.britannica.com/topic/Mithraism.

Motala, Tasnim. "The Genocide Name Game: The Case for Crimes Against Humanity to Prevent Genocide." *Quinnipiac Law Review* 37 (2019): 611.

Mt. Healthy City School District Board Of Education v. Doyle, 429 U.S. 274, 287, 97 S. Ct. 568, 50 L. Ed. 2D 471 (1977).

Nemo, Stephen Z. "Jihadi Cool: Hip Hop Earns its Bad Rap." *Communities Digital News*, August 26, 2014. Accessed June 1, 2024. http://www.commdiginews.com/politics-2/commentary/jihadi-cool-hip-hop-earns-its-bad-rap-24622/.

Nietzsche, Friedrich. *Jenseits von Gut und Böse. Zur Genealogie der Moral (1886)*, edited by Giorgio Colli and Mazzino Montinari. Munich, Germany: dtv Verlagsgesellschaft mbH & Co KG, 1999, reprint 2002.

Papke, David Ray. "Myth and Meaning: Francis Ford Coppola and Popular Response to the Godfather Trilogy." In *Legal Reelism: Movies as Legal Texts*, edited by John Denvir, 1–22. Champaigne, Illinois: University of Illinois Press, 1996.

Patel, Faiza. "Rethinking Radicalization." *Brennan Center for Justice at the N.Y.U. School of Law*, March 8, 2011. https://www.brennancenter.org/publication/rethinking-radicalization.

Pearson, Elizabeth. "Macho Cool: The Appeal of Violent Jihad." *Connect Justice Blog*, September 30, 2013. https://web.archive.org/web/20131001074900/http:/www.connectjustice.org/blog.php?d=3.

Picart, Caroline Joan "Kay" S. *American Self-Radicalizing Terrorists and the Allure of "Jihadi Cool/Chic."* Newcastle upon Tyne: Cambridge Scholars Publishing, 2017.

Picart, Caroline Joan "Kay" S. "Jihad Cool/Jihad Chic: The Roles of the Internet and Imagined Relations in the Self-Radicalization of Colleen LaRose (Jihad Jane)." *Societies 5* (April 2015): 354–83. doi:10.3390/soc5020354.

Picart, Caroline Joan "Kay" S. "Monstrous Discourses, Jihadi Cool, and Emergent Counter-Terrorist Narratives: The Case of Ahmad Khan Rahami (a.k.a. Ahmad Rahimi) and the 2016 New York/New Jersey Bombings." In *Monsters, Law, Crime: Explorations in Gothic Criminology*, edited by Caroline Joan "Kay" S. Picart, 245–80. Madison: Fairleigh Dickinson University Press, 2021.

Picart, Caroline Joan "Kay" S.. "Nationalities, Histories, Rhetorics: Real/Reel Representations of the Holocaust and Holocaust Trials and a Poethics of Film and Law." *Dapim: Studies on the Holocaust* 29, no. 2 (May 2015): 17–19.

Picart, Caroline Joan "Kay" S. and David A. Frank. *Frames of Evil: The Holocaust as Horror in American Film*. Carbondale: Southern Illinois University Press, 2006.

Pizler, Reid C. "Essay: Peace is not the Absence of Conflict, but the Presence of Justice." *NIU Law Review* 29, no. 2 (2009): 335–424.

Porter, R.C. "'Jihad Cool'—Young Americans Lured to Fight for ISIS Militants; Seeds of Next 9/11?" *Fortuna's Corner*, June 28, 2014. https://web.archive.org/web/20180609070132/http:/fortunascorner.com/2014/06/28/jihad-cool-young-americans-lured-to-fight-for-isis-militants-seeds-of-next-911/.

Press Release. "Senate Homeland Security Committee Hearing Examines Islamic Radicalism Inside United States." *Senate Committee on Homeland Security and Governmental Affairs*, March 14, 2007. https://web.archive.org/web/20110311211755/http:/hsgac.senate.gov/public/index.cfm?FuseAction=Press.MajorityNews&ContentRecord_id=d0543abb-0376-4a5c-9a4e-09649e2ed8ef.

Press Release. "What's Radicalizing Muslim Americans?" *Homeland Security Committee* (Peter King), December 19, 2010. Accessed June 1, 2024. http://homeland.house.gov/press-release/newsday-king-whats-radicalizing-muslim-americans.

Prosecutor v. Akayesu, ICTR Trial Judgment, 2 September 1998, para. 513.

Prosecutor v. Gacumbitsi, ICTR Trial Judgment, 17 June 2004, para. 255

Prosecutor v. Jelisić, ICTY Appeals Judgment, 5 July 2001, para. 49.

Prosecutor v. Kaing (alias Duch), ECCC Trial Judgment, 26 July 2010, para. 342

Prosecutor v. Kajelijeli, ICTR Trial Judgment, 1 December 2003, para. 813.

Prosecutor v. Karadžić, ICTY Trial Judgment, 24 March 2016, para. 6049.

Prosecutor v. Karadžić et al, Review of the Indictment Pursuant to Rule 61 of the Rules of Procedure and Evidence, 11 July 1996, para. 93.

Prosecutor v. Katanga, ICC Trial Judgment, 7 March 2014, para. 975 and para. 977

Prosecutor v. Kayishema et. al., ICTR Trial Judgment, 21 May 1999, para. 116.

Prosecutor v. Krnojelac, ICTY Trial Judgment, 15 March 2002, para. 329.

Prosecutor v. Krstić, ICTY Appeals Judgment, 19 April 2014, para. 25-26.

Prosecutor v. Krstić, ICTY Trial Judgment, 2 August 2001, para. 513.

Prosecutor v. Kunarac, ICTY Appeals Judgment, 12 June 2002, para. 119.

Prosecutor v. Kunarac, ICTY Trial Judgment, 22 February 2001, para. 542.

Prosecutor v. Kupreskić, ICTY Trial Judgment, 14 January 2000, para. 594.

Prosecutor v. Muhimana, ICTR Trial Judgment, 28 April 2005, para. 500.

Prosecutor v. Musema, ICTR Trial Judgment, 27 January 2000, para. 161.

Prosecutor v. Rutaganda, ICTR Trial Judgment, 6 December 1999, para. 51.

Prosecutor v. Stakić, ICTY Appeals Judgment, 31 July 2003, para. 25.

Prosecutor v. Stakić, Trial Judgment, 31 July 2003, para. 516.

Prosecutor v. Tadic, ICTY Trial Judgment, 7 May 1977, paras. 704–710.

Prosecutor v. Tolimir, ICTY Appeals Judgment, 8 April 2015, para. 209.

Prosecutor v. Tolimir, ICTY Trial Judgment, 12 December 2012, para. 756.

Pyke v. Cuomo, 258 F.3d 107, 109 (2d Cir. 2001).

Quinney, Richard. "Who Is The Victim?" *Criminology* 10, no. 3 (November 1972): 314–23.

Rabasa, Angel, Stacie L. Pettyjohn, Jeremy J. Ghez, and Christopher Boucek. "Deradicalizing Islamist Extremists." *Rand Corporation Arlington Virginia National Security Research Division*, 2010. https://www.ojp.gov/ncjrs/virtual-library/abstracts/deradicalizing-islamist-extremists.

"Radicalization, Information Sharing and Community Outreach: Protecting the Homeland from Homegrown Terror." Hearing Before the Senate Committee on Intelligence, Information Sharing, and Terrorism Risk Assessment of the House Committee on Homeland Security, 110th Cong. 2 (2007) (testimony of John Neu, Chief of Police Dep't). Accessed June 1, 2024. http://hsc-democrats.house.gov/SiteDocuments/20070405120653-23987.pdf.

Raza v. City of New York, 998 F. Supp. 2D 70 (E.D.N.Y. 2013).

Reeson, Greg C. *Stalemate: Why We Can't Win the War on Terror and What We Should Do Instead*. Lanham: Government Institutes, 2011.

ReligionForBreakfast. "Yazidi Religion Explained." YouTube video, September 10, 2020, 18:18. https://www.youtube.com/watch?v=QRB9e9Ol4Hs.

Republic of Croatia v. Republic of Serbia, Application of the Convention on the Prevention and Punishment of the Crime of Genocide, ICJ Judgment, 3 February 2015, paras. 362–364.

"The Role of Local Enforcement in Countering Violent Islamic Extremism." Hearing Before the Senate Committee on Homeland Security and Governmental Affairs, 110th Cong. 1 (2007) (statement for the record by Maj. Thomas Dailey, Kansas City, Mo. Police Department, Homeland Security Division). Accessed June 1, 2024. http://hsgac.senate.gov/public/index.cfm?FuseAction=Files.View&FileStore_id=81c0387a-e20c-4b02-8257-6885b0e1c3f5.

"Rome Statute of the International Criminal Court." *United Nations Office of Legal Affairs*, July 17, 1998. https://legal.un.org/icc/statute/99_corr/cstatute.htm.

Rosen v. Thornburgh, 928 F.2d 528, 533 (2d Cir. 1991).

Roussinos, Aris. "Jihad Selfies: These British Extremists in Syria Love Social Media." *Vice.com*, December 5, 2013. http://www.vice.com/read/syrian-jihadist-selfies-tell-us-a-lot-about-their-war.

Rushdie, Salman. "'Jihadi cool' Language Luring Britons to Islamic State." *Haaretz*, October 11, 2014. http://www.haaretz.com/news/middle-east/1.620223.

Russell-Brown, Sherrie L. "Rape as an Act of Genocide." *Berkeley Journal of International Law* 21, no. 2 (2003): 350–74.

Sageman, Marc. *Leaderless Jihad: Terror Networks in the Twenty-First Century.* Philadelphia: University of Pennsylvania Press, 2008.

Saleh, Heba. "Western Female Jihadis Deploy 'Soft-Power' of Isis Online." *Financial Times*, October 28, 2014. http://www.ft.com/cms/s/0/2d8b020c-5792-11e4-8493-00144feab7de.html.

Savir, Aryeh. "ISIS Teen CRISIS: Jihadist Recruitment of American Kids." *United with Israel*, October 29, 2014. http://unitedwithisrael.org/isis-teen-crisis-jihadist-recruitment-of-american-kids/.

Scherbakovskiy v. Da Capo Al Fine, Ltd., 490 F.3d 130, 138 (2d Cir. 2007).

Schmitt, Eric. "In Battle to Defang ISIS, U.S. Targets Its Psychology." *New York Times*, December 28, 2014. http://www.nytimes.com/2014/12/29/us/politics/in-battle-to-defang-isis-us-targets-its-psychology-.html?_r=0.

Shneer, David. *Through Soviet Jewish Eyes: Photography, War, and the Holocaust.* New Brunswick: Rutgers University Press, 2012.

Silber, Mitchell D. and Arvin Bhatt. "Radicalization in the West: The Homegrown Threat." *New York City Police Department* (2007): 57–82. Accessed June 1, 2024. http://www.nyc.gov/html/nypd/downloads/pdf/public_information/NYPD_Report-Radicalization_in_the_West.pdf.

Silke, Andrew. "Holy Warriors: Exploring the Psychological Processes of Jihadi Radicalization." *European Journal of Criminology* 5, no. 1 (2008): 99–123.

Tarbush, Susannah. "New British Initiatives Aim to Counter ISIS on Social Media." *The Tanjara*, August 28, 2015.

"'They Came To Destroy': ISIS Crimes Against the Yazidis." *United Nations Human Rights Council*, Thirty-second session, Agenda Item 4, Human Rights Situations that Require the Council's Attention, June 15, 2016. https://www.ohchr.org/sites/default/files/Documents/HRBodies/HRCouncil/CoISyria/A_HRC_32_CRP.2_en.pdf

Tomlinson, Simon and Tom McTague. "ISIS Want to Impregnate Yazidi Women and Smash Our Bloodline': Fears Grow for the 300 Women Kidnapped from Sinjar." *MailOnline*, August 14, 2014. https://www.dailymail.co.uk/news/article-2724658/Were-not-leaving-Yazidis-refusing-come-mountain-300-women-stolen-ISIS-impregnated-smash-blond-bloodline.html.

U.N. General Assembly, UDHR [Universal Declaration of Human Rights], Article 1; Preamble.

"UN Human Rights Panel Concludes ISIL Is Committing Genocide Against Yazidis." *UN News Centre*, June 16, 2016.

United Parcel Service Of America, Inc. v. The Net. Inc., 222 F.R.D. 69,71 (E.D.N.Y. 2004).

United States v. Armstrong, 517 U.S. 456, 465, 116 S. Ct. 1480, 134 L. Ed. 2D 687 (1996).

United States v. Avery, 137 F.3d 343, 352 (6th Cir. 1997).

United States v. City of Yonkers, 96 F.3d 600, 611–12 (2d Cir. 1996).

United States v. Scopo, 19 F.3d 777, 786 (2d Cir. 1994) (Newman, C.J., concurring).

Usher, Barbara Plett. "The US State Department's YouTube 'Digital Jihad.'" *BBC*, November 28, 2014. http://www.bbc.com/news/magazine-30045038.

Vago, Steven and Ben Kesslen. "Salman Rushdie Attacker Praises Iran's Ayatollah, Surprised Author Survived: Jailhouse Interview." *New York Post*, August 17, 2022. https://nypost.com/2022/08/17/alleged-salman-rushdie-attacker-didnt-think-author-would-survive/.

van Dijck, José. *The Culture of Connectivity: A Critical History of Social Media*. New York: Oxford University Press, 2013.

Van Schaak, Beth. "Engendering Genocide: The Akayesu Case Before the International Criminal Tribunal for Rwanda." Legal Studies Research Paper Series, Santa Clara University School of Law, July 2008.

Village Of Arlington Heights v. Metropolitan Housing Development Corporation, 429 U.S. 252, 270, 97 S. Ct. 555, 50 L. Ed. 2D 450 (1977).

"Violent Extremism: How Are People Moved from Constitutionally-Protected Thought to Acts of Terrorism?" Hearing Before Senate Select Committee on Intelligence, Information Sharing and Terror Risk Assessment of the Hearing Before the House Committee on Homeland Security, 111th Congress, 3 (2009) (testimony of Kim Cragin, RAND Corporation).

Walker, Theresa. "Has ISIS Reached O.C.? Arrest Here Intensifies Questions." *Orange County Register*, August 30, 2014. http://www.ocregister.com/articles/dandach-633351-isis-orange.html.

Ward, M.L. "Second American Jihadi Confirmed Dead in ISIS." *Uptown Magazine*, August 29, 2014. https://web.archive.org/web/20151024033701/https:/www.uptownmagazine.com/2014/08/second-american-jihadi-confirmed-dead-isis/2/.

Weimann, Gabriel. "New Terrorism and New Media." *Wilson Center: Research Series*, volume 2, 2014. https://www.wilsoncenter.org/sites/default/files/media/documents/publication/STIP_140501_new_terrorism_F.pdf.

Weisberg, Richard. *Poethics and Other Strategies of Law and Literature*. New York: Columbia University Press, 1992.

Westcott, Lucy. "Amal Clooney Says U.N. has Failed Yazidi Women." *Newsweek*, September 17, 2016.

The White House. *Statement by the President.* August 7, 2014. https://obamawhitehouse.archives.gov/the-press-office/2014/08/07/statement-president.

Whren v. United States, 517 U.S. 806, 813, 116 S. Ct. 1769, 135 L.E. 89 (1996).

"Why did Isis Attack the Yezidi People?" *CBS News*, May 8, 2016. https://www.cbsnews.com/news/60-minutes-overtime-why-did-isis-attack-the-yezidi-people/

Yoon, Carol Kaesuk. "Stephen Jay Gould, 60, Is Dead; Enlivened Evolutionary Theory." *New York Times*, May 21, 2002. https://www.nytimes.com/2002/05/21/us/stephen-jay-gould-60-is-dead-enlivened-evolutionary-theory.html.

Index

About the Author

Caroline Joan "Kay" S. Picart is a distinguished scholar-lawyer, with an MPhil from the University of Cambridge-Christ's College (as the Sir Run Run Shaw Scholar and Wolfson Prize Winner); a PhD in social and political philosophy (with doctoral minors in aesthetics, criticism, and comparative literature) from Pennsylvania State University; a postdoctoral scholar at the Cornell School of Criticism and Theory (in jurisprudence); and joint juris doctor in law (*cum laude*, with certificates in international law and intellectual property), and MA in women's studies (Tybel Spivack Teaching Fellow), University of Florida.

Currently, Caroline is an appeals attorney at the Florida Tenth Judicial Circuit's Public Defender's Office. Prior to that, in 2018, Caroline established her own firm focusing on Criminal Law, Family and Property Law, while also serving as a Special Assistant Public Defender with the Public Defender's Office, Tenth Judicial Circuit since 2015. At the University of Florida Levin College of Law, she served as Editor-in-Chief of the *Florida Journal of International Law*; under her leadership, *FJIL* caught up with two backlogged issues and published three additional issues, raising the journal's profile to among the top international law journals. Simultaneously, she served as Communications Executive and was an Articles Editor, Research Editor, and Communications Executive, at different times, of the *Journal of Technology Law & Policy*.

As a Florida Bar Foundation Fellow at the Florida Institutional Legal Services, Caroline had an inside look at what legal advocacy entails. Similarly, her externship and pro bono work under the State Attorney's Office in the Eighth Circuit complemented that experience with perspective from the opposing side. As a Postgraduate Public Interest Fellow at the Eighth Judicial Circuit Court, Caroline assisted various criminal law and civil law judges, and focused mainly on assisting a senior staff attorney with the disposition of prisoner petitions, complaints, and motions, including the initial evaluation of :w cases, research of legal issues, and preparation of proposed orders.

Prior to establishing her own practice, Caroline served as an Of Counsel appellate attorney to a Tampa-based federal criminal defense firm and a Gainesville-based Family Law firm. She has successfully advocated for numerous clients on various issues inclusive of timeshare, alimony, child support, and parental relocation in Family Law. She has also been a fierce advocate for numerous clients in Criminal Law felony direct appeals and in relation to postconviction relief. Caroline believes that the three most important qualities in an attorney working with individuals undergoing a divorce are: (1) compassion, (2) competence, and (3) commitment. She knows that first, divorces, even when they are amicable, are disruptive, not only for the individuals but also particularly for young children; thus, she believes that the ability to connect and communicate compassionately is important in establishing trust and rapport with a client. Second, while being compassionate is essential, she believes competence in the practice of law is important in negotiating or advocating for the best possible results for clients. For her, competence includes the ability to think creatively and innovatively in formulating legal strategies or arguments, tempered by both experience and a pragmatic grounding. Third, she believes that commitment to both the client and, as a practicing member of the Florida Bar, to the legal community, is crucial to balancing the demands of advocacy with ethical and professional obligations to the larger legal community.

Caroline has an impressive record of publications in legal (and philosophy, film, sociology, communications, criminology, among other) journals and scholarly, refereed monographs and edited collections, and continues to publish actively and collaborate with both national and international experts on law and crime, as well as intellectual property and property, both within US and international contexts. She has received numerous awards, among which was the prestigious 2016 "Best Essay Award" by *Dapim*, an international scholarly journal on Holocaust studies in Israel. She was an invited speaker to a NATO-sponsored Advanced Research Workshop on Lone Wolf Terrorism in Jerusalem, Israel, and has been an invited speaker to several law schools on US copyright, international intellectual property, and US self-radicalizing terrorism. She brings this international and critical perspective to her cases and enjoys the attentiveness to detail, the vividness of narrative, and rigorous logical reasoning the practice of law requires. She has memberships/court admissions in Florida State courts and the US District Court, Southern and Middle Districts of Florida, and was an adjunct professor at the Florida A & M University College of Law, where she taught Family Law. Prior to her career in law, she was a tenured professor of philosophy, film, and humanities with a courtesy appointment at a law school. She has helped numerous students with recommendations for higher education degrees and jobs, and has mentored them in the process of professionalizing.

Caroline adores her beloved Puerto Rican husband, Gerardo "Jerry" Rivera, their resident Bengal, Calico, and German Shepherd, and is deeply devoted to her Filipino, Tallahassean, and Puerto Rican families. She was a US Open Ballroom Champion in Cabaret (a mix of ballroom, ballet, and gymnastics), and enjoys social dancing with her husband. She has also exhibited her fine point pen drawings and oil and mixed media paintings in various galleries and venues in the Philippines, South Korea, and various parts of the United States. In 2005, she started her own fine art and ballroom dance company, Kinaesthetics, LLC, which continues to be active. Internationally, she was invited to be a features writer for the *Korea Times* and *Filipinas Magazine*. Prior to proceeding to law school, she hosted and produced a radio show, which, at the time she closed the show, was carried by fifty-nine national and international affiliates (an estimated listenership of over two million monthly listeners, nationally and internationally). As a first-generation Filipino immigrant to the U.S., she is bilingual in English and Filipino, and has some literacy in Spanish and German.

www.ingramcontent.com/pod-product-compliance
Ingram Content Group UK Ltd.
Pitfield, Milton Keynes, MK11 3LW, UK
UKHW020208290926
15470UKWH00001B/58

9 781683 934387